Speak Japanese!

日本人がよく使う
日本語会話
お決まり表現

180 Common Expressions
Used by Native Japanese
Speakers in Regular Conversation

180

清ルミ 著
Sei Rumi

Jリサーチ出版

Japanese has many useful rhetorical expressions that fully convey a specific nuance through a single term. These expressions are known by all Japanese people and are generally used without a second thought, yet they are rarely discussed in Japanese textbooks. Also, basic verbs and adjective introduced in JLPT N4- and N5-level textbooks are often used with different meanings than how they are described in these books.

This book features some of the basic expressions among these that are particularly used frequently in daily life. I have divided 180 expressions into 26 categories to make it easy for you to find the expression that communicates what you want to say. The meaning, background, and usage of the expressions are also introduced.

Inside this book, you will also find 50 mini-columns about expressions that use basic vocabulary in ways that are unlike the meanings you may have seen in your textbooks. I have tried to give you easy-to-understand conversational situations and example sentences, and believe you will be able to easily understand the situations and manner in which these expressions should be used.

Please use this book to further enrich your expressive skills in Japanese.

Rumi Sei

　日本語には、たった一言でニュアンスがしっかり伝わる便利なレトリック表現がたくさんあります。日本人なら誰もが知っていて、普段なにげなく使っているものですが、そのような表現は、日本語の教科書ではあまり紹介されていません。また、日本語能力試験のＮ４〜Ｎ５レベルの基本的な動詞や形容詞が、教科書で紹介されている意味とは違う意味で使われることもよくあります。

　そこで、この本では、これらの表現の中から特に生活の中でよく使われる基本的なものを取り上げました。言いたいことを伝える表現を見つけやすいよう、180の表現を26のカテゴリーに分けて、意味や背景説明、使い方を紹介してあります。

　初級の語彙を教科書とは違う意味で使った表現も、50のミニコラムで紹介しました。わかりやすい会話場面と例文を心がけましたので、どんな状況でどんなふうに使うのか、容易にご理解いただけると思います。

　この本で、あなたの日本語の表現力をますます豊かなものにしてください。

清ルミ

Table of Contents
目次
もくじ

Section A	When things are going well / fortunately	20

順調な様子、ラッキーなこと
じゅんちょう ようす

1 楽勝 No problem; a breeze らくしょう	2 朝飯前 Piece of cake; a cinch あさめしまえ
3 棚ぼた Windfall; godsend たな	4 お安い御用 No big deal; piece of cake やす ごよう
5 トントン拍子 Without a hitch; びょうし swimmingly	6 一番乗り First to arrive いちばんの

Section B	Efficient things, doing things efficiently	26

効率的なこと、効率的に事を進める
こうりつてき こうりつてき こと すす

7 一石二鳥 Two birds with one stone いっせきにちょう	8 善は急げ Strike while the iron is hot ぜん いそ
9 先手を打つ Beat to the punch せんて う	10 根回し Lay the groundwork; ねまわ consensus-building

Section C	To have a strong interest, to become serious	30

強い関心を持つ、本気になる
つよ かんしん も ほんき

11 ハマる Get hooked	12 目がない Have a weakness for; be a め sucker for
13 病みつき To be addicted to; hooked や	14 我を忘れる Forget oneself; lose oneself われ わす
15 首を突っ込む Stick your nose in くび つ こ	16 本腰を入れる Put your back into ほんごし い

Section D	Knowing the truth, understanding the situation	36

本当のことがわかる、状況を理解する
ほんとう じょうきょう りかい

17 目からウロコ Scales falling from eyes め	18 空気を読む Read the atmosphere/ くうき よ situation

How to Use This Book
この本の使い方

The expressions in this book are split into 26 sections (A to Z) based on their unique traits.

表現の特徴から 26 のセクション (A ～ Z) に分けられています。

This is the expression discussed on this page. There are 180 expressions in total. ——

このページで取り上げている表現です。表現は全部で 180 あります。

"Listen & Speak" ——

Two examples of dialogues or monologues are introduced.

会話またはモノローグの例を 2 つ紹介しています。

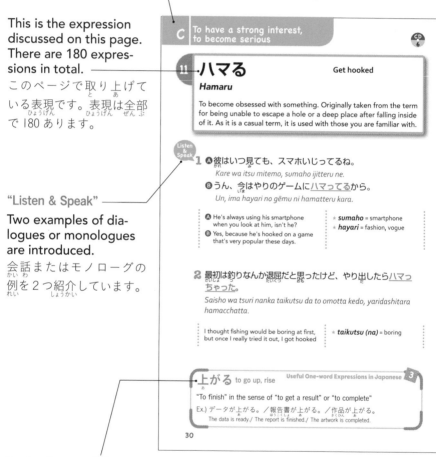

C To have a strong interest, to become serious

CD 6

11 **ハマる** Get hooked

Hamaru

To become obsessed with something. Originally taken from the term for being unable to escape a hole or a deep place after falling inside of it. As it is a casual term, it is used with those you are familiar with.

Listen & Speak

1 Ⓐ彼はいつ見ても、スマホいじってるね。
Kare wa itsu mitemo, sumaho ijitteru ne.

Ⓑうん、今はやりのゲームにハマってるから。
Un, ima hayari no gēmu ni hamatteru kara.

Ⓐ He's always using his smartphone when you look at him, isn't he?
Ⓑ Yes, because he's hooked on a game that's very popular these days.

＊ **sumaho** = smartphone
＊ **hayari** = fashion, vogue

2 最初は釣りなんか退屈だと思ったけど、やり出したらハマっちゃった。
Saisho wa tsuri nanka taikutsu da to omotta kedo, yaridashitara hamacchatta.

I thought fishing would be boring at first, but once I really tried it out, I got hooked

＊ **taikutsu (na)** = boring

上がる to go up, rise　Useful One-word Expressions in Japanese **3**

"To finish" in the sense of "to get a result" or "to complete"

Ex.) データが上がる。／報告書が上がる。／作品が上がる。
The data is ready./ The report is finished./ The artwork is completed.

30

Useful One-word Expressions in Japanese

Fifty beginner words are singled out in order to discuss meanings and usage that differ from what you may have learned in your textbook. Learn these, as they are frequently used in conversation. (Mini-columns, 50 in total)

初級単語から 50 語を取り上げ、教科書で習うのとは別の意味や使い方を紹介します。ふだんの会話でよく使われるもので、ぜひ覚えておきたいものです。
(ミニコラム・全 50 回)

An expression's basic meaning, background, usage scenario, and more is explained.
基本的な意味や背景、使われる場面などを解説
きほんてき　いみ　はいけい　つか　ばめん　かいせつ
しています。

The section this page belongs to is highlighted.
このページのあるセクション
を濃くしています。
こ

C 強い関心を持つ、本気になる
つよ　かんしん　も　ほんき

12 目がない
め
Me ga nai

Have a weakness for; be a sucker for

To like something unconditionally. Primarily used for food and drink. Often used when thanking someone for a gift you have received. *Be careful, as 「～を見る目がない」 means "Does not properly judge something's value."

Listen & Speak

1 Ⓐ これ、京都の和菓子です。
きょうと　わがし
　　Kore, Kyōto no wagashi desu.

　Ⓑ ありがとう！甘いものに<u>目がない</u>からうれしいです。
あま　め
　　Arigatō! Amai mono ni me ga nai kara ureshī desu.

Ⓐ These are Japanese sweets from Kyoto.
Ⓑ Thank you! I have a weakness for sweets.

★ **wagashi** = Japanese confection
★ **amai mono** = sweets

Vocabulary that some may find difficult is singled out and explained.
少し難しい語句などを取
すこ　むずか　ごく　と
り上げ、説明しています。
あ　せつめい

2 Ⓐ 彼は日本酒に<u>目がない</u>みたいだから、お歳暮はお酒がいいと思うよ。
かれ　にほんしゅ　め　せいぼ　さけ　おも
　　Kare wa nihonshu ni me ga nai mitai da kara, o-sēbo wa o-sake ga ī to omou yo.

　Ⓑ そうですか。じゃあ、そうします。
　　Sō desu ka. Jā, sō shimasu.

Ⓐ He seems to have a weakness for sake, so I think you should get him some as an end-of-year gift.
Ⓑ Is that so? Then I'll do that.

★ **o-sēbo** = year-end gift

31

Information on how to download voice information can be found in the back of this book.
音声ダウンロードの案内は、本の一番後ろの部分にあります。
おんせい　あんない　ほん　いちばんうし　ぶぶん

11

How to use the CD
ＣＤの使い方

CD

The attached CD includes the titles of each unit as well as recordings of all of the "Listen & Speak" conversation examples introduced in them (in Japanese only).

付属 CD には、各ユニットのタイトルと「Listen & Speak」で紹介している会話例がすべて収録されています（ともに日本語のみ）。

1: Begin by quickly reading over the conversation. Imagine the scene in which the conversation is taking place and understand what is being said.

2: Next, take a look at the book while listening to the CD. Imagine how the speakers feel as you hear them talk. As you confirm how each expression is used, also pay attention to details in how the words are being spoken, such as the speaker's accent and intonation.

3: Look at the book and read aloud the conversations while imitating the speakers in the CD.

4: Listen to the CD without looking at the book and understand what is being said. Also try repeating after the CD as you listen to it.

❶ まず最初に、会話文をざっと読んでみましょう。会話が行われている場面をイメージしながら、意味を理解しましょう。

❷ 次に、本を見ながら CD を聴きましょう。話している人がどんな気持ちか、想像しながら聞いてください。また、アクセントやイントネーションなど、音のニュアンスにも注意しながら、その表現がどのように使われるか、確認しましょう。

❸ 本を見ながら、CD の音をまねるように、声に出して読んでみましょう。

❹ 本を見ないで聴いて、意味を理解しましょう。また、CD の音を追いかけるように口に出して言ってみましょう。

Introduction◆
Figures of Speech in Japanese
which Convey a Nuance in Just
One Word

序章◆たった一言でニュアンスが伝わる
日本語のレトリック表現

Expressions that is indispensable to a conversationy

会話に欠かせない便利な表現

Among the expressions used by speakers of Japanese in their daily lives, there are some very useful "one-word expressions which, once you know them, can be used to convey your feelings and thoughts, as well as what you have seen and heard, with accuracy and with subtle nuance". A large number of expressions of this nature are known as "figures of speech*" or "rhetorical figures".

* These are verbal techniques such as metaphor and personification, emphasis such as repetition and anastrophe, as well as onomatopoeia and imitative words.

"Figures of speech" may sound rather abstract and difficult, but in fact, they are so important that, without them, natural speech would be impossible. Indeed, they are used very often in everyday speech and conversation.

There are figures of speech in English, too. Take the world-famous song, *"You Are My Sunshine"*. The loved one is compared to sunshine and the title conveys not only the strength of the singer's feelings but also the wonderful qualities of the loved one.

As for Wall Street, it is not just the name of a place. It also signifies the center of finance which controls economic trends in America. The United States Department of Defense is known as the Pentagon because of the five-sided building in which it is housed. This is also a figure of speech.

普段、日本人が使っている表現の中には、「たった一言、これを知っていたら、人の気持ちや考え、見たこと聞いたことなどを、さまざまなニュアンスを込めて的確に相手に伝えることができる」という、とても便利な表現があります。このような表現の多くがレトリック＊表現と呼ばれるものです。

＊比喩や擬人法、反復や倒置などの強調、擬音語・擬態語など、さまざまな表現の技法。

レトリックというと、抽象的で難しいもののように聞こえるかもしれませんが、実は、これがなければ自然な会話が成り立たないほど大切なものなのです。実際、日常のことばのやりとりの中で、非常に多く、頻繁に使われています。

英語にもレトリック表現があります。"You are my sunshine"という世界中で有名な歌がありますね。愛する恋人を太陽にたとえたことで、恋人への愛情の強さや恋人がどんなに素敵な人かが伝わる題名です。Wall streetと言えば、単なる地名ではなく、アメリカ経済の動向を左右する金融の中心を意味します。アメリカの国防総省を、建物が五角形であることからPentagon（五角形）と呼ぶのもレトリックの一つです。

15

Your conversation becomes rich and enjoyable

会話が楽しく、豊かなものになる

The advantage of using figures of speech is that by using the form and nature of familiar objects as examples, we can make ourselves understood quickly and easily. People have, since long ago, devised new expressions not only out of necessity, but also for the joy of using language. If we say that a sentence consisting merely of words used one after the other is black and white, then we can say that one which includes figures of speech is colourful and classy.

Let us take the example of two people who are hostile to each other and whose bad relationship is clear to those around them. If we describe those two people using ordinary adjectives and verbs, we will need a long sentence, like the one above. If, however, we know and can use the expression [犬猿の仲] (a dog and monkey relationship), we can dispense with superfluous explanation. We can understand the relationship immediately with just this one expression. Thus, conversation becomes not only easy to understand, but also enjoyable and fresh.

このように、ある物事やそれに対する感情を表現するのに、身近なものの形や性質などにたとえることで、相手にすんなりと理解してもらえるのがレトリック表現の利点です。レトリック表現は、昔から人々が必要にかられて行ってきた言葉の工夫であり、言葉の楽しみ方でもあります。単語を並べた説明的な表現がモノクロの表現だとすれば、レトリック表現は、彩り豊かなおしゃれな表現だといえます。

たとえば、とても仲が悪くて、互いによく思っていないことが周囲からも明らかな、険悪な雰囲気の二人がいたとしましょう。この二人のことを、普通の形容詞や動詞を使って表現しようとすれば、前の文のように長い描写が必要です。しかし、「犬猿の仲」という表現を知っていて、使うことができたら、余分な説明は一切いりません。この表現だけで、二人の関係がすぐに理解されます。会話がわかりやすくなるだけでなく、より楽しく、生き生きとしたものになります。

Japanese power of expression increases
日本語の表現力が高まる

There are many action verbs in Japanese which are used to express behaviour or emotion in Japanese figures of speech. An example is 「首を突っ込む」(to stick one's neck out), to indicate strong interest by exaggerating the appearance of stretching one's neck forward. The expression 「あぐらをかく」, which means sitting with one's legs crossed, conveys arrogant behaviour. Also, when we meet with unexpected luck, we can use the humorous expression 「棚ぼた（棚からぼたもち）」, which means that sweet rice and bean cakes have happened to fall off a shelf. In this way, we can use visual descriptions to express our feelings accurately, as if we were watching a film. It is a creative way to play with the language.

Once you have learnt and can use figures of speech, your scope in the language will really increase and your ability to express yourself in Japanese and your command of the language will improve dramatically. Without a doubt, you will gain confidence in conversing and will feel you can brag a bit to others.

日本語のレトリック表現には、動作を表す動詞を使って態度や心情を表す表現もたくさんあります。たとえば、強い関心を示す心理状態を、首が前のめりになる格好を誇張して、「首を突っ込む」と表現します。何かに対して横柄な態度をとることは、「あぐらをかく」と、脚を開いたくだけた座り方の描写で表現します。また、予期しないラッキーなことに出合ったことは、「棚ぼた（＝棚からぼたもち）」と、棚から甘い菓子が偶然落ちてきたと、ユーモラスに表現します。このように、動画を見ているかのようなわかりやすい視覚的描写を用いることで、心の状態を的確に表現できるのです。これはまさに芸術的な言葉の遊びです。

このようなレトリック表現を覚えて使えるようになれば、会話の幅がグンと広がり、日本語の表現力や運用力が飛躍的に高まります。会話に自信を持つことができ、ちょっと人に自慢できるような気持ちになること、間違いなしです。

180 Expressions Used by Native Japanese Speakers in Regular Conversation

日本人がよく使う
日本語会話お決まり表現 180

楽勝
らくしょう
Rakushō

No problem; a breeze

Something that can be done easily or with resources to spare. The term comes from the idea of "an easy win." Used with those you are close with. Often used after receiving a request as a considerate way not to put psychological pressure on the person receiving the request.

Listen & Speak

1 Ⓐ これ、悪いけど、明日までにやってくれないかな？

Kore, waruikedo, asu madeni yattekurenai kana?

Ⓑ わかりました。金曜日までなら楽勝です。

Wakarimashita. Kin'yōbi made nara rakushō desu.

- Ⓐ Sorry, but could you do this by tomorrow?
- Ⓑ Understood. Doing this by Friday will be no problem.

- ★ *~madeni* = by ~
- ★ *warui kedo ....* = I'm sorry, but....

2 Ⓐ バスだとわかりませんが、タクシーを使えば 15 分で楽勝ですよ。

Basu dato wakarimasen ga, takushī o tsukaeba 15-fun de rakushō desu yo.

Ⓑ そうですか。じゃあ、そうします。

Sō desu ka. Jā, sō shimasu.

- Ⓐ I don't know about taking a bus, but you should be able to get there with no problem in fifteen minutes if you take a taxi.
- Ⓑ Is that so. I'll do that, then.

- ★ *X de rakushō (≒ x de raku ni ~ dekiru)* = can ~ in/by/with X

2 朝飯前
あさめしまえ
Asameshimae

Piece of cake; a cinch

Something that can be done easily. A metaphor for something that can be done so easily that it can even be done on an empty stomach, before eating breakfast. Often used when accepting someone's request without any hesitation.

1 Ⓐ えっ、毎日 20 キロ走ってるんですか。
まいにち　　　　はし

Ett, mainichi 20-kiro hashitteru n desu ka?

Ⓑ はい。そのぐらい<u>朝飯前</u>ですよ。
あさめしまえ

Hai. Sonogurai asameshimae desu yo.

Ⓐ What? You run twenty kilometers a day?
Ⓑ Yes. That much is a piece of cake.

★ ***kiro*** = kilometer(s)
★ ***sonogurai (soregurai)*** = like that, that much

---

2 Ⓐ この問題、解ける人、誰かいないかなあ。
もんだい　と　　ひと　だれ

Kono mondai, tokeru hito, dareka inai kanā.

Ⓑ 関さんならきっと<u>朝飯前</u>だと思いますけど。
せき　　　　　　　あさめしまえ　　　おも

Seki-san nara kitto asameshimae da to omoimasu kedo.

Ⓐ Can anyone solve this problem?
Ⓑ It's probably a piece of cake for Seki-san.

★ ***toku*** = solve (tokeru=can solve)

緑 green
みどり

Useful One-word Expressions in Japanese 1

Nature, vegetation, plants

Ex.) この辺は緑が多い。／緑を増やす計画
へん　みどり　おお　　みどり　ふ　　けいかく

There's a lot of greenery here. / a plan to increase the amount of vegetation

3 棚ぼた
たな
Tana-bota

Windfall; godsend

A *bota-mochi* (Japanese sweet given as an offering to deceased ancestors) falling from a shelf. A metaphor that means "To come across unexpected good fortune."

1 Ⓐ友だちからもらったくじでハワイ旅行が当たっちゃった！
とも　　　　　　　　　　　　　　　　りょこう　　あ
Tomodachi kara moratta kuji de Hawai ryokō ga atacchatta!

Ⓑすごい！　まさに棚ぼただね、それは。
たな
Sugoi! Masani tana-bota dane, sore wa.

Ⓐ I won a trip to Hawaii from the lottery ticket my friend gave me!
Ⓑ Wow! What a windfall.

★ *kuji* = lot
★ *~ga ataru* = win ~

2 Ⓐ今月の営業成績、随分いいねえ。
こんげつ　えいぎょうせいせき　ずいぶん
Kongetsu no ēgyō-sēseki, zuibun ī nē.

Ⓑはい。ライバル店が閉店したので、棚ぼたで急に客が増えたんです。
てん　へいてん　　　　　　　　　たな　　　きゅう　きゃく　ふ
Hai. Raibaru-ten ga hēten shita node, tana-bota de kyūni kyaku ga fueta n desu.

Ⓐ This month's sales results are quite good.
Ⓑ Yes. Our rival store closed, and we had a windfall rush of customers.

★ *ēgyōsēseki* = sales result, business performance
★ *zuibun* = pretty, a lot, a good deal

4

お安い御用
やす ご よう
O-yasui go-yō

No big deal; piece of cake

To be able to accept someone's request without any difficulty to oneself. This expression is used to set at ease someone who feels bad for making a request. The「安い」does not refer to a low price, but means easily done, or simple.「御用」is used because someone else's business is being discussed, causing the honorific「御」to be used.

1 Ⓐ あのう、この荷物、5時頃まで預かってもらえませんか。
にもつ じ ごろ あず

Anō, kono nimotsu, 5-ji goro made azukatte moraemasen ka?

Ⓑ いいですよ。<u>お安い御用</u>です。
やす ご よう

Ī desu yo. O-yasui goyō desu.

Ⓐ Um, could you please hold on to this luggage until around 5?

Ⓑ Sure. No big deal.

★ **azukaru** = keep

2 Ⓐ いつもすみません、無理なお願いばかりして。
む り ねが

Itsumo sumimasen, murina onegai bakari shite.

Ⓑ 大丈夫ですよ。このくらい<u>お安い御用</u>ですよ。
だいじょう ぶ やす ご よう

Daijōbu desu yo. Kono kurai o-yasui go-yō desu yo.

Ⓐ I'm sorry for always making these unreasonable requests.

Ⓑ It's fine. This is no big deal.

★ **muri(na)** =unreasonable, difficult

★ **onegai** = request, asking

5 # トントン拍子
びょう　し
Tonton-byōshi

Without a hitch; swimmingly

For something to proceed smoothly. This term comes from the idea of an actor making lively steps on a stage in time with a teacher's clapping.

1 Ⓐあれ？　彼はもう部長になったの？
かれ　　　　ぶちょう

Are? Kare wa mō buchō ni natta no?

Ⓑそうなんです。<u>トントン拍子</u>の出世ですよね。
びょう　し　　しゅっ せ

Sō na n desu. Tonton-byōshi no shusse desu yo ne.

Ⓐ Huh? He's already department chief?
Ⓑ That's right. His advancement up the ranks has been going swimmingly.

★ **buchō** = general manager, division manager
★ **shusse** = career success

---

2 Ⓐあの二人はうまく行ってるんですか。
ふた り　　　　　い

Ano futari wa umaku itteru n desu ka?

Ⓑええ、交際を始めてから<u>トントン拍子</u>で、来年には結婚す
こうさい　はじ　　　　　　　びょう し　　　らいねん　　　けっこん

るようです。

Ē, kōsai o hajimete kara tonton-byōshi de, rainen niwa kekkon suru yō desu.

Ⓐ Are those two getting along well?
Ⓑ Yes, things have been going without a hitch ever since they started seeing one another, and it seems they'll be married next year.

★ **umaku iku** = go well
★ **kōsai** = dating, relationship

---

6 一番乗り
いちばん の
Ichiban-nori

First to arrive

To be the first to arrive in a given location. Originally used to refer to someone being the first on the battlefield to ride a horse into an enemy position. To be the first to attack.「乗る」means "to be the first to head into a given location, or to be the first to succeed."
の

1 Ⓐ 会場に一番乗りしたのは社長だって。
かいじょう いちばん の しゃちょう
Kaijō ni ichiban-nori shita nowa shachō date.

Ⓑ そうなんだ。

Sō na n da.

Ⓐ I heard the president was the first to arrive at the site.
Ⓑ Really?

★ **kaijō** = venue, site

2 Ⓐ サッカーの結果、どうだった？
けっか
Sakkā no kekka, dō datta?

Ⓑ 日本、勝ったよ。ワールドカップの出場、一番乗りだって。
に ほん か しゅつじょう いちばん の
Nihon, katta yo. Wārudokappu no shutsujō, ichiban-nori da tte.

Ⓐ How did the soccer match go?
Ⓑ Japan won. I heard they're the first team to make it to the World Cup.

★ **kekka** = result
★ **shutsujō** = participation, appearance, entry

Useful One-word Expressions in Japanese **2**

悪い bad
わる

申し訳ない to be sorry
もう わけ

Ex.) 忙しい時に頼んで、悪いですね。／悪いけど、これ持って。
いそが とき たの わる わる も
I'm sorry to ask you when you're so busy. / Sorry, but hold this.

7 一石二鳥

<ruby>一<rt>いっ</rt></ruby><ruby>石<rt>せき</rt></ruby><ruby>二<rt>に</rt></ruby><ruby>鳥<rt>ちょう</rt></ruby>

Isseki-nichō

Two birds with one stone

To get multiple results from a single action. A metaphor based on the idea of throwing a single stone and bringing down two birds.

1 **Ⓐ** 節約のためにお酒を飲みに行くのを半分にしたら、５キロ減ったよ。

Setsuyaku no tameni o-sake o nomi ni iku no o hanbun ni shitara, 5-kiro hetta yo.

Ⓑ へえ。ダイエットとお金の節約で一石二鳥ですね。

Hē. Daietto to o-kane no setsuyaku de isseki-nichō desu ne.

> **Ⓐ** When I started drinking only half as often in order to save money, I lost five kilograms.
> **Ⓑ** Wow. You dieted and saved money. That's two birds with one stone.

> ★ ***setsuyaku(suru)*** = saving (money)

2 早起きはいいですよ。健康的だし使える時間が増えるし、一石二鳥ですよ。

Hayaoki wa ī desu yo. Kenkōteki dashi, tsukaeru jikan ga fueru shi, isseki-nichō desu yo.

> Waking up early is good. It's healthy and you have more time you can use. It's two birds with one stone.

> ★ ***hayaoki*** = early rising
> ★ ***kenkōteki (na)*** = healthy

8 善は急げ
ぜん　　いそ
Zen wa isoge

Strike while the iron is hot

A suggestion to not wait and to act immediately if something seems good. Often used when giving advice to someone or urging them to action.

1 Ⓐ えっ、タバコ捨てちゃうの？　開けてないじゃない。
す　　　　　　　　　あ
Ett, tabako sutechau no? Aketenai janai.

Ⓑ うん、禁煙しようと決めたから。<u>善は急げ</u>って言うでしょ？
きんえん　　　　き　　　　　　ぜん　いそ　　　　い
Un, kin'en shiyō to kimeta kara. Zen wa isoge tte yū desho?

Ⓐ What? You're going to throw away those cigarettes? You didn't even open them.	★ **suteru** =throw away ★ **kin'en suru** = stop smoking
Ⓑ Yes, I decided I'm going to quit smoking. Strike while the iron is hot, right?	

2 部長、この案絶対いいですよ。すぐ取り掛かりましょう。<u>善は</u>
ぶ ちょう　　　あんぜったい　　　　　　　と　か　　　　　　　　ぜん
<u>急げ</u>、ですから。
いそ
Buchō, kono an zettai ī desu yo. Sugu torikakarimashō. Zen wa isoge, desu kara.

I think that plan is definitely a good one, boss. Let's get started on it immediately. Strike while the iron is hot, after all!	★ **an** = plan, idea ★ **zettai** = definitely, absolutely ★ **torikakaru** = begin, set about

9 先手を打つ
せんてうつ
Sente o utsu

Beat to the punch

To come up with a countermeasure for something before others can come up with their own measure. Strategies in matches of go and *shogi* are known as 「手」. The phrase is a metaphor based on attacking your opponent before he can attack you. Often used in business settings.

1 **Ⓐ** 向こうはどういう金額を出してくるでしょう。
むこう きんがく だ
Mukō wa dōyū kingaku o dashitekuru deshō?

Ⓑ 先手打って、こっちの希望の額を伝えようか。
せんてう きぼう がく つた
Sente utte, kocchi no kibō no gaku o tsutaeyō ka?

> **Ⓐ** I wonder how much money they're going to quote us.
> **Ⓑ** Why don't we beat them to the punch and tell them the price we want?

> ★ **mukō** = they
> ★ **kingaku (gaku)** = amount (of money)

2 **Ⓐ** また、あいつに先手を打たれちゃった。
せんて う
Mata, aitsu ni sente o utarechatta.

Ⓑ えっ、また？ のんびりしてるからだよ。
Ett, mata? Nonbiri shiteru kara da yo.

> **Ⓐ** He beat me to the punch again.
> **Ⓑ** What, again? It's because you are too easygoing.

> ★ **nonbiri suru** = feel at ease, feel easy, relax

10 根回し
Nemawashi
ね　まわ

Lay the groundwork; consensus-building

To obtain unofficial consent beforehand from participants who will attend a meeting so that approval can be smoothly attained during the official meeting. From the horticultural term for trimming a tree's roots prior to transplanting it in order to increase the number of small roots. Often used in business settings or in meetings with others.

1 Ⓐ あの企画、無事通りましたね。
きかく　　ぶじとお
Ano kikaku, buji tōrimashita ne.

Ⓑ そりゃ、そうだよ。しっかり根回ししといたからね。
ね　まわ
Sorya, sō da yo. Shikkari nemawashi shitoita kara ne.

Ⓐ That plan was approved without an issue.

Ⓑ Of course it was. We made sure to lay all the groundwork first.

★ **kikaku** =plan, planning, project

★ **buji (bujini)** = without any trouble

2 Ⓐ 反対意見出ないように、昼休みに根回ししておこう。
はんたいいけんで　　　　　ひるやすみ　　ね　まわ
Hantai iken denai yō ni, hiruyasumi ni nemawashi shiteokō.

Ⓑ そうだね。そのほうが安全だね。
あんぜん
Sō da ne. Sono hō ga anzen da ne.

Ⓐ We should do some consensus-building during our lunch break so that no dissenting opinions come up.

Ⓑ You're right. It would be safer that way.

★ **hantai iken** = dissenting opinion

★ **anzen (na)** = safe

11 # ハマる

Hamaru

Get hooked

To become obsessed with something. Originally taken from the term for being unable to escape a hole or a deep place after falling inside of it. As it is a casual term, it is used with those you are familiar with.

Listen & Speak

1 Ⓐ 彼はいつ見ても、スマホいじってるね。
Kare wa itsu mitemo, sumaho ijitteru ne.

Ⓑ うん、今はやりのゲームに<u>ハマってる</u>から。
Un, ima hayari no gēmu ni hamatteru kara.

Ⓐ Whenever you see him, he's always fiddling with his smartphone, isn't he?

Ⓑ Yes, because he's hooked on a game that's very popular these days.

★ **sumaho** = smartphone
★ **hayari** = fashion, vogue

2 最初は釣りなんか退屈だと思ったけど、やり出したら<u>ハマっちゃった</u>。

Saisho wa tsuri nanka taikutsu da to omotta kedo, yaridashitara hamacchatta.

I thought at first that fishing would be boring, but once I tried it, I got hooked.

★ **taikutsu (na)** = boring

上がる to go up, rise   **Useful One-word Expressions in Japanese** 3

"To finish" in the sense of "to get a result" or "to complete"

Ex.) データが上がる。／報告書が上がる。／作品が上がる。
The data is ready./ The report is finished./ The artwork is completed.

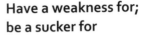

12

目がない
め
Me ga nai

**Have a weakness for;
be a sucker for**

To like something unconditionally.
Primarily used for food and drink. Often
used when thanking someone for a gift
you have received. *Be careful, as 「〜を
見る目がない」 means "Does not properly
み　　め
judge something's value."

**Listen
& Speak**

1

Ⓐ これ、京都の和菓子です。
　　　　きょうと　わがし

　　Kore, Kyōto no wagashi desu.

Ⓑ ありがとう！甘いものに<u>目がない</u>からうれしいです。
　　　　　　　あま　　　　　め

　　Arigatō! Amai mono ni me ga nai kara ureshī desu.

Ⓐ These are Japanese sweets from Kyoto.

Ⓑ Thank you! I have a weakness for sweets.

★ **wagashi** = Japanese confection

★ **amai mono** = sweets

2

Ⓐ 彼は日本酒に<u>目がない</u>みたいだから、お歳暮はお酒がいい
　　かれ　にほんしゅ　　め　　　　　　　　　せいぼ　　さけ
　　と思うよ。
　　　おも

　　*Kare wa nihonshu ni me ga nai mitai da kara, o-sēbo wa o-sake
　　ga ī to omou yo.*

Ⓑ そうですか。じゃあ、そうします。

　　Sō desu ka. Jā, sō shimasu.

Ⓐ He seems to have a weakness for sake, so
I think you should get him some as an end-
of-year gift.

Ⓑ Is that so? Then I'll do that.

★ **o-sēbo** = year-end gift

Ⓐ When things are going well / Fortunately

Ⓑ Efficient things, doing things efficiently

Ⓒ To have a strong interest, to become serious

Ⓓ Knowing the truth, understanding the situation

Ⓔ To not be bothered, to not be worried, to feel relieved

Ⓕ Doing something kindly, thoroughly, gently, and steadily

Ⓖ To strongly desire, to crave

Ⓗ Dodging something so that it is more convenient for you

Ⓘ To influence

13 病みつき
Yamitsuki

To be addicted to; hooked

To be so obsessed with something that you cannot quit it. Originally taken from a term that means "To fall ill, or to be in a state where you are starting to fall ill." Used with those you are close with.

1 〈ランチタイムに〉
〈ranchitaimu ni〉

Ⓐ また、そのカップラーメン？

Mata, sono kappurāmen?

Ⓑ うん。一度食べたら病みつきになっちゃって。

Un. Ichido tabetara, yamitsuki ni nacchatte.

Ⓐ (During lunch) You're eating those cup noodles again?

Ⓑ Yes. I got addicted to them after the first time I ate them.

★ *kappurāmen* = cup noodles

---

2 彼女を競馬に連れてったら、もう病みつき。今では僕より競馬場に通ってるよ。

Kanojo o kēba ni tsuretettara, mō yamitsuki. Imadewa boku yori kēbajō ni kayotteru yo.

I took her to the horse races once and now she's hooked. She goes to the track more often than me now.

★ *kēba* = horse race
★ *tsuretettara* ⇐ *tsureteittara* *tsureteiku* = take (someone)

---

14 # 我を忘れる
われ わす
Ware o wasureru

Forget oneself; lose oneself

To become so excited that you lose track of time and rationality, becoming engrossed or obsessed about something.

Ⓐ When things are going well / fortunately

Ⓑ Efficient things, doing things efficiently

Ⓒ To have a strong interest, to become serious

Ⓓ Knowing the truth, understanding the situation

Ⓔ To not be bothered, to feel relieved

Ⓕ Doing something kindly, thoroughly, gently, and steadily

Ⓖ To strongly desire, to crave

Ⓗ Dodging something so that it is more convenient for you

Ⓘ To influence

1 Ⓐ アトリエに入ると、我を忘れて絵を描いちゃうんだ。
はい われ わす え か

Atorie ni hairuto, ware o wasurete e o kaichau n da.

Ⓑ へー、そうなんだ。

Hē, sō na n da.

Ⓐ When I enter my studio, I forget myself and just start painting.
Ⓑ Huh, is that so?

★ **atorie** = atelier
★ **kaichau** ⇐ kaiteshimau

2 Ⓐ なんでそんなことしたの？

Nande sonna koto shita no?

Ⓑ 家族のこと悪く言われたから、怒りで我を忘れちゃったんだよ。
か ぞく わる い いか われ わす

Kazoku no koto waruku iwareta kara, ikari de ware o wasurechatta n da yo.

Ⓐ Why did you do something like that?
Ⓑ They said something bad about my family, so I forgot myself in my anger.

★ **ikari** = anger

CD 8

15

首を突っ込む
くび　つ　こ
Kubi o tsukkomu

Stick your nose in

To become strongly interested or involved in something. Often used when describing someone's excessive actions in a critical way, or when advising them to be careful.

Listen & Speak

1 Ⓐ あまり人のことに<u>首を突っ込まない</u>方がいいと思うけど。
ひと　　　　　　　　くび　つ　こ　　　　　ほう　　　　　　　おも

Amari hito no koto ni kubi o tsukkomanai hō ga ī to omou kedo.

Ⓑ そうだけど。つい気になっちゃって。
き

Sō da kedo. Tsui ki ni nacchatte.

Ⓐ You shouldn't stick your nose into other people's affairs too much.

Ⓑ Yes, that's true, but I was just so interested.

★ *ki ni naru* = be concerned, worry

2 彼、政治に<u>首を突っ込み</u>過ぎて、新しい仕事もやめちゃったら
かれ　せいじ　　くび　つ　こ　す　　　　　あたら　しごと

しいよ。

Kare, sēji ni kubi o tsukkomisugite, atarasī shigoto mo yamechatta rashī yo.

He has his stuck nose so far into politics that it sounds like he quit his new job.

★ *yameru* = quit

熱い hot
あつ

Useful One-word Expressions in Japanese **4**

Passionate, very enthusiastic

Ex.) 熱く話す／あの人は熱い。／熱い気持ち
あつ　はな　　　　　ひと　あつ　　　　あつ　き　も
To talk with ardour / That person is very enthusiastic./ ardent feeling

16 本腰を入れる
ほんごし い
Hongoshi o ireru

Put your back into

To become serious as you tackle something. 「腰」 is often used to
describe one's stance toward something.
こし

Listen & Speak

1 Ⓐ そろそろ試験勉強に本腰入れないとね。
しけんべんきょう ほんごし い
Sorosoro shiken-benkyō ni hongoshi irenai to ne.

Ⓑ そうだね。あと一か月しかないからね。
いっ げつ
Sō da ne. Ato ikkagetsu shika nai kara ne.

Ⓐ It's about time to put my back into test preparation.
Ⓑ Yes, there's only a month left, after all.

★ **sorosoro** = it is about time to ~

2 Ⓐ ほんとに９月までに間に合うかなあ。
がつ ま あ
Honto ni ku-gatsu made ni maniau ka nā.

Ⓑ 大丈夫だよ、これから本腰入れてやれば。
だいじょうぶ ほんごし い
Daijōbu da yo, korekara hongoshi irete yareba.

Ⓐ Will we really make it by September?
Ⓑ It's fine, just as long as we start putting our backs into it.

★ **ma ni au** = be in time

冷たい cold
つめ

Useful One-word Expressions in Japanese 5

Cold-hearted, without sympathy or kindness

Ex.) 冷たい人／冷たい態度
つめ ひと つめ たいど
A cold person / cold attitude

17 目からウロコ

Me kara uroko

Scales falling from eyes

Used when the truth about something is learned or when something unclear is then clarified. The phrase comes from a story in the New Testament, and while the Japanese translates literally to "Scales from eyes," the actual saying is "Scales falling from eyes."

Listen & Speak

1 **Ⓐ** 昨日の講演会どうだった？

Kinō no kōenkai dō datta?

Ⓑ すごくよかったよ。目からウロコの話がいっぱい聞けた。

Sugoku yokatta yo. Me kara uroko no hanashi ga ippai kiketa.

Ⓐ How was yesterday's lecture?

Ⓑ It was incredible. I heard a lot of things that made it feel like the scales were falling from my eyes.

★ **kōenkai** = lecture, lecture meeting

2 〈説明を聞いて〉

へー、そうだったんですか。それは知りませんでした。目からウロコです。知らない人、多いと思います。

〈*Setsumē o kīte*〉

Hē, sō datta n desu ka. Sore ha shirimasen deshita. Me kara uroko desu. Shiranai hito, ōi to omoimasu.

〈After hearing an explanation〉

Oh, so that's what it was? I never knew that. It's like the scales have fallen from my eyes. I think a lot of people don't know that.

★ **setsumē** = explanation

18
空気を読む
くう　き　　よ
Kūki o yomu

Read the atmosphere/ situation

To understand the feeling or situation of a location, then to deduce how others feel before taking appropriate actions. This is also often used in a negative manner, such as 「空気が読めない人」.
くう　き　　よ　　　　　ひと

A When things are going well / fortunately

B Efficient things, doing things efficiently

C To have a strong interest to become serious

D Knowing the truth, understanding the situation

E To not be bothered, to not be worried, to feel relieved

F Doing something kindly, thoroughly, gently, and steadily

G To strongly desire, to crave

H Dodging something so that it is more convenient for you

I To influence

1 **Ⓐ** じゃ、それ、僕がやりますよ。
ぼく

Ja, sore, boku ga yarimasu yo.

Ⓑ ちょっとぉ。もう少し空気読みなよ。その仕事は田中さん
すこ　　　　くうき　よ　　　　　　　しごと　たなか
がずっとやりたがってたんだから。

Chottō. Mō sukoshi kūki yomina yo. Sono shigoto wa Tanaka-san ga zutto yaritagatteta n da kara.

> **Ⓐ** Okay, then I'll do it.
> **Ⓑ** Hold on a second. Read the situation here a little better. Tanaka-san has wanted to do that job for a long time.

> ★ *~(shi) tagaru* = be anxious to ~, be eager to ~

2 **Ⓐ** 石田さんはほんとに空気読めないよね。
いし だ　　　　　　　　　　くう き　よ

Ishida- san wa honto ni kūki yomenai yo ne.

Ⓑ うん。なんでわからないのかなあ。

Un. Nande wakaranai no ka nā.

> **Ⓐ** Ishida-san really can't read a situation, can he?
> **Ⓑ** Yes. I wonder why he can't figure it out?

> ★ *nande (= dōshite, naze)* = why

19 # ダメ元
もと
Dame-moto

Nothing to lose

An abbreviation of "Lost from the beginning." To recognize that something is impossible but to still hold slight hope that one will be happy if things goes well.

Listen & Speak

1 Ⓐ ダメ元で講演をお願いしたら、ＯＫとれたよ。
もと こうえん ねが
Damemoto de kōen o o-negai shitara, ōkē toreta yo.

Ⓑ えーっ、あの中村先生が来てくれるの!?
なかむらせんせい き
Ētt, ano Nakamura-sensē ga kite kureru no!?

Ⓐ I asked her to give a lecture since there was nothing to lose, and she said okay.

Ⓑ What? You mean Nakamura-sensei is going to give us a lecture?!

★ **kōen** = lecture talk

2 Ⓐ えっ、ふじホテル、土曜日じゃ、部屋がとれないんじゃない？
どようび へや
Ētt, Fuji-hotel, doyōbi ja, heya ga torenai n ja nai?

Ⓑ まあ、ダメ元で電話してみます。
もと でんわ
Mā, dame-moto de denwa shite mimasu.

Ⓐ Huh? Isn't it impossible to get a hotel room at the Fuji Hotel on a Saturday?

Ⓑ Well, I don't have anything to lose. I'll try calling them.

★ **heya o toru**
(=heya o yoyaku suru)
= reserve a room

20 安全パイ
あんぜん
Anzen-pai

Safe Tile; safe choice

A passable person or selection that will neither benefit nor harm anyone. This refers to dealing a tile in mahjong that no other player can use to win.

1 Ⓐ 彼女を家まで送るのは森君がいいんじゃない？
かのじょ　いえ　　　おく　　　　もりくん

Kanojo o ie made okuru no wa Mori-kun ga ī n ja nai?

Ⓑ そうだね。彼なら<u>安全パイ</u>だし。
かれ　　　あんぜん

Sō da ne. Kare nara anzen-pai da shi.

Ⓐ Shouldn't Mori-kun be the one to walk her home?

Ⓑ You're right. He's a safe tile, after all.

★ *~ made okuru* = see (someone) to ~

2 Ⓐ どっちのプランがいい？

Docchi no puran ga ī?

Ⓑ そうだね。いま赤字だから、こっちの方が<u>安全パイ</u>かもね。
あかじ　　　　　　　　　　ほう　　あんぜん

Sō da ne. Ima akaji da kara, kocchi no hō ga anzen-pai kamo ne.

Ⓐ Which plan do you prefer?

Ⓑ Well, we're in the red right now, so this one would probably be the safer choice.

★ *akaji* = deficit

揺れる **to shake**
ゆ

Useful One-word Expressions in Japanese 6

迷う to be unsure
まよ

Ex.) 心が揺れる。／どっちにするか、まだ揺れています。
こころ　ゆ　　　　　　　　　　　　　　　ゆ

To be indecisive. / I still don't know which one to choose.

21 痛くもかゆくもない
いた
Itaku mo kayuku mo nai

No skin off my nose; don't even notice

To cause no trouble at all, to not be at all influenced

1 Ⓐ ゆうべまた、田中さんにごちそうになっちゃいました。
たなか

  Yūbe mata, Tamaka-san ni gochisō ni natchaimashita.

Ⓑ いいんじゃない？ 彼は株でもうけてるから、それぐらい
かれ かぶ
<u>痛くもかゆくもない</u>よ。
いた

  Ī n ja nai? Kare wa kabu de mōketeru kara, sore gurai itaku mo
  kayuku mo nai yo.

Ⓐ Tanaka-san ended up paying for dinner again last night.

Ⓑ Isn't that fine? He's making money in the stock market, so it must be no skin off his nose to be able to spend that kind of money.

★ **yūbe** = last evening, evening
★ **mōkeru** = make money, gain

---

2 Ⓐ B評価か……。私だったら、ちょっとがっかりだけど、別
ひょうか わたし べつ
に<u>痛くもかゆくもない</u>んでしょ？
いた

  Bī-hyōka ka …. Watashi dattara, chotto gakkari da kedo, betsu
  ni itak mo kayuku mo nai n de sho?

Ⓑ まあね。

  Mā ne.

Ⓐ B rating? I'd personally be a little depressed by it, but it's not like it's any skin off your nose, is it?

Ⓑ I guess not.

★ **hyōka** = valuation
★ **gakkari** = be dissapointed

---

22 肩の荷が下りる
かた　に　　お
Kata no ni ga oriru

A weight lifted from your back

To be freed of some responsibility, anxiety, or burden.

1 Ⓐ監督、優勝おめでとうございます！
かんとく　　ゆうしょう
Kantoku, yushō omedetō gozaimasu!

Ⓑありがとうございます。これで、やっと肩の荷が下りました。
かた　に　お
Arigatō gozaimasu. Korede, yatto kata no ni ga orimashita.

Ⓐ Congratulations on the victory, director!

Ⓑ Thank you very much. This has finally lifted a big weight off my back.

★ **kantoku** = head coach, director, supervisor

2 Ⓐお嬢さんの結婚が決まって、肩の荷が下りたんじゃないで
じょう　　　けっこん　き　　　　　　　　かた　に　お
すか。
O-jō-san no kekkon ga kimatte, kata no ni ga orita n ja nai desu ka?

Ⓑほんとにそう。ホッとしました。
Honto ni sō. Hotto shimashita.

Ⓐ Hasn't a lot been taken off your back now that your daughter is going to be married?

Ⓑ It really has. I breathed a sigh of relief.

★ **o-jō-san** (=a polite expression of one's daughter)
★ **hotto suru** = be relieved

23 # 手とり足とり
てあし

Te tori ashi tori

Attention to detail

To handle something down to the last detail in a thorough, kind, and proper way. Metaphor for taking someone's hands and legs while properly teaching them something.

1 Ⓐ あそこのパソコン教室、どう？
きょうしつ

Asoko no pasokon-kyōshitsu, dō?

Ⓑ うん、先生が親切だよ。手とり足とり教えてくれるからね。
せんせい　しんせつ　　　て　　あし　おし

Un, sensē ga shinsetsu da yo. Te tori ashi tori oshiete kureru kara ne.

Ⓐ How is that computer school?
Ⓑ The teacher is kind. She teaches you with a lot of attention to detail.

★ **pasokon** = (personal) computer

2 私が日本に来たばかりの頃、ホストファミリーがいろいろ手とり足とり教えてくれました。そのおかげで早く日本の生活に慣れることができました。
わたし　にほん　き　　　　ころ　　　　　　　　　　　　　　て　あし　おし　　　　　　　　　　　　　　　　はや　にほん　せいかつ　な

Watashi ga Nihon ni kita bakari no koro, hosuto-famirī ga iroiro te tori ashi tori oshiete kuremashita. Sono okage de hayaku Nihon no sēkatsu ni nareru koto ga dekimashita.

When I first came to Japan, my host family taught me many things with attention to detail. Thanks to that, I was able to quickly get used to life in Japan.

★ **~(shi) tabakari** = have just ~(p.p.)
★ **~no okage de** = thanks to ~

42

24 一から十まで
Ichi kara jū made

From A to Z

To do absolutely everything properly. More often said about others than about yourself. A straightforward way of saying this is "Everything from the beginning to the end."

Listen & Speak

1 Ⓐ料理、上手ですね。どこかで習ったんですか。
　　Ryōri. jōzu desu ne. Doko ka de naratta n desu ka?

Ⓑいえ。料理は一から十まで母に教えてもらったんです。
　Ie. Ryōri wa ichi kara jū made haha ni oshiete moratta n desu.

Ⓐ You're a good cook. Did you study cooking somewhere?

Ⓑ No, my mother taught me how to cook from A to Z.

★ **ryōri** = cooking

2 Ⓐ彼はちょっと面倒。一から十まで説明しないと納得しないから。
　　Kare wa chotto mendō. Ichi kara jū made setsumē shinai to nattoku shinai kara.

Ⓑそうなんだ。
　Sō na n da.

Ⓐ He's a bit of a pain. He won't be satisfied unless you explain everything from A to Z.

Ⓑ Is that so?

★ **mendō (na)** = troublesome
★ **nattoku suru** = be convinced, accept

Ⓐ When things are going well / fortunately
Ⓑ Efficient things, doing things efficiently
Ⓒ To have a strong interest, to become serious
Ⓓ Knowing the truth, understanding the situation
Ⓔ To not be bothered, to not be worried, to feel relieved
Ⓕ Doing something kindly, thoroughly, gently, and steadily
Ⓖ To strongly desire, to crave
Ⓗ Dodging something so that it is more convenient for you
Ⓘ To influence

25 かゆいところに手が届く

Kayui tokoro ni te ga todoku Extremely thorough

To be considerate and thoughtful to the point that one addresses details that most usually would not. Often used as a complement.

Listen & Speak

1 Ⓐ いつも同じホテルだね。

Itsumo onaji hoteru da ne.

Ⓑ うん、ここはサービスいいからね。かゆいところに手が届く感じで。

Un, koko wa sābisu ī kara ne. Kayui tokoro ni te ga todoku kanji de.

Ⓐ You always stay at the same hotel.

Ⓑ Yes, because the service is good here. They're extremely thorough.

★ **sābisu** = service

---

2 Ⓐ ねえ見て。こんなところにもポケットがついてるよ。

Nē mite. Konna tokoro ni mo poketto ga tsuiteru yo.

Ⓑ ほんとだ。かゆいところに手が届いてるね。

Honto da. Kayui tokoro ni te ga todoiteru ne.

Ⓐ Hey, look. There's even a pocket here.

Ⓑ You're right. They're extremely thorough, aren't they?

★ **poketto** = pocket

見えない can't see | Useful One-word Expressions in Japanese 7

Can't confirm easily, can't grasp well

Ex.) 話が見えない。／結果が見えない。
I can't understand what was said. / I can't predict the result.

26 コツコツ

Untiringly; steadily

Kotsu-kotsu

Used to describe steady and solid efforts toward a goal. A straightforward way to say this is "To tackle something in a steady and solid way."

1 Ⓐ お仕事をやめた後、何かしたいことありますか。
しごと　　　　あと　なに

O-shigoto o yameta ato,nanika shitai koto arimasuka?

Ⓑ 海外旅行かな？　<u>コツコツ</u>貯めてきたお金であちこち行き
かいがいりょこう　　　　　　　　　た　　　　　　かね　　　　　　　い
たいね。

Kaigai-ryokō ka na? Kotsu-kotsu tametekita o-kane de achikochi ikitai ne.

- Ⓐ Is there anything you want to do after you leave your job?
- Ⓑ Travel overseas, maybe. I want to use some of the money I untiringly saved to go all around.

- ★ **tameru** = save
- ★ **achikochi** = here and there

2 Ⓐ 彼女、合格したんだ。やっぱり<u>コツコツ</u>努力してきた人は
かのじょ　ごうかく　　　　　　　　　　　　　どりょく　　　　　　ひと
違うね。
ちが

Kanojo, gōkaku shita n da. Yappari kotsu-kotsu doryoku shite kita hito wa chigau ne.

Ⓑ そうだね。

Sō da ne.

- Ⓐ So she passed. People who work toward something untiringly really are different.
- Ⓑ Yes, you're right.

- ★ **chigau** = different (from others)

CD 14

27 〜に飢える
~ni ueru

Starving for ~

To desire something even more because it has been unattainable for so long.

Listen & Speak

1

Ⓐ 捨て猫を拾ってきたんだけど、くっついて離れないんだ。
Suteneko o hirotte kita n da kedo, kuttsuite hanarenai n da.

Ⓑ よほど愛情に飢えてたんだろうね。
Yohodo aijō ni ueteta n darō ne.

Ⓐ I picked up an abandoned cat, but it won't leave my side now.

Ⓑ It must have been starved for affection.

★ **kuttsuku** = stick
★ **aijō** = love, affection

2

Ⓐ〈入院見舞いに本をもらって〉

ありがとう！ 活字に飢えてたから嬉しいよ。
〈*Nyuin mimai ni hon o moratte*〉
Arigatō! Katsuji ni ueteta kara ureshī yo.

Ⓑ 本好きだから、そうじゃないかな、と思って。
Honzuki da kara, sō ja nai ka na, to omotte.

Ⓐ〈After receiving a book from a hospital visitor〉

Thank you! I was starved for some reading material. This makes me happy.

Ⓑ I thought so, since you love books.

★ **katsuji** = printing type, books or magazines (⇐ printed matter)
★ **ureshī** = be glad

28 喉から手が出るほど欲しい
のど て で ほ

Nodo kara te ga deru hodo hoshī

Want desperately

A way of directly expressing an unbearable desire for something.

Listen & Speak

1 Ⓐ いいなあ。これ、<u>喉から手が出るほど欲しい</u>よ。
のど て で ほ

Ī nā. Kore, nodo kara te ga deru hodo hoshī yo.

Ⓑ 私だって何年も節約して、やっと手に入れたんだから。
わたし なんねん せつやく て い

Watashi datte nan-nen mo setsuyaku shite, yatto te ni ireta n da kara.

Ⓐ This is so nice. I desperately want it.
Ⓑ I had to save for years to finally get one myself.

★ **setsuyaku suru** = save money
★ **te ni ireru** = get

2 Ⓐ 彼は本当にすばらしい選手だね。
かれ ほんとう せんしゅ

Kare wa hontō ni subarashī senshu da ne.

Ⓑ うん。うちのチームに<u>喉から手が出るほど</u>欲しいよ。
のど て で ほ

Un. Uchi no chīmu ni nodo kara te ga deru hodo hoshī yo.

Ⓐ He really is a wonderful player, isn't he?
Ⓑ Yes. I desperately want him on our team.

★ **subarashī** = wonderful

うそ a lie

Useful One-word Expressions in Japanese 8

Is that true?

Ex.)「明日は雨だよ」「うそ！」／「これ、1000円だった」「えっ、うそ！」
あした あめ えん

"It's going to rain tomorrow." "Really?" / "This cost ¥1,000." "Really? Wow!"

Ⓐ When you are going to wait / fortunately

Ⓑ Efficient things, doing things efficiently

Ⓒ To have a strong interest to become serious

Ⓓ Knowing the truth, understanding the situation

Ⓔ To not be bothered, to be worried, to feel relieved

Ⓕ Doing something kindly, thoroughly, gently, and steadily

Ⓖ To strongly desire, to crave

Ⓗ Dodging something so that it is more convenient for you

Ⓘ To influence

29 # 首を長くして待つ
くび　なが　　　　ま

Look forward to

Kubi o nagaku shite matsu

Expresses the state of continuing to look forward to something and hoping it comes soon.

1 Ⓐ お嬢さん、留学先から戻ってきましたか。
　　じょう　　りゅうがくさき　　もど

　O-jō-san, ryūgaku-saki kara modotte kimashita ka?

Ⓑ ええ、やっと。どれだけ<u>首を長くして待った</u>かわかりませ
　　　　　　　　　　　　　　くび　なが　　　　ま
んよ。

　Ē, yatto. Doredake kubi o nagaku shite matta ka wakarimasen yo.

Ⓐ Has your daughter returned from studying abroad?

Ⓑ Yes, at last. I can't tell you how much I was looking forward to her coming back.

★ *~saki* = the place where one will do / did something to, someone that one will do / did something to

2 Ⓐ 合格通知、<u>首長くして待ってる</u>んだけど、ちっとも届かな
　　ごうかくつうち　くびなが　　　　ま　　　　　　　　　　とど
いんだ。

　Gōkaku-tsūchi, kubi nagaku shite matteru n da kedo, chittomo todokanai n da.

Ⓑ 大丈夫よ。きっと届くから。
　　だいじょうぶ　　　　　とど

　Daijōbu yo. Kitto todoku kara.

Ⓐ I'm really looking forward to receiving my acceptance notice, but it's not showing up at all.

Ⓑ It's fine, I'm sure you'll get one.

★ *tsūchi* = notice
★ *chittomo ~ nai* = not at all ~

30 待ちに待った
まま
Long-awaited

Machi ni matta

Said when something you have waited on and expected for a long time finally arrives. Nouns such as things or people come after the expression.

1 Ⓐやった！　明日から待ちに待った夏休みだ！
あした まま なつやす

Yatta! Ashita kara machi ni matta natsuyasumi da!

Ⓑお疲れさま。リフレッシュしてきてくださいね。
つか

O-tsukare-sama. Rifuresshu shite kite kudasai ne.

Ⓐ Yay! Our long-awaited summer break starts tomorrow!

Ⓑ You've worked hard. Take the opportunity to recharge yourself.

★ *rifuresshu suru* = refresh oneself

2 Ⓐなんだかテンション高いですね。
たか

Nandaka tenshon takai desu ne.

Ⓑそりゃ、そうですよ。今夜は待ちに待った彼女とのデートですからね。
こんや まま かのじょ

Sorya sō desu yo. Kon'ya wa machi ni matta kanojo to no dēto desu kara ne.

Ⓐ You seem excited.

Ⓑ Of course I am. Tonight is my long-awaited date with my girlfriend.

★ *nandaka (=nazedaka, nazeka)* ~ = I don't know why, but ~

Ⓐ When things are going well / doing things efficiently

Ⓑ Efficient things, doing things efficiently

Ⓒ To have a strong interest to become serious

Ⓓ Knowing the truth, understanding the situation

Ⓔ To not be bothered, to not be worried, to feel relieved

Ⓕ Doing something kindly, thoroughly, gently, and steadily

Ⓖ To strongly desire, to crave

Ⓗ Dodging something so that it is more convenient for you

Ⓘ To influence

31 ごまをする

Goma o suru

Butter up

To flatter or praise someone to get on their good side for your own gain.

Listen & Speak

1 Ⓐ 最近ずっと忙しくしているから、たまには女房のゴマすって、ケーキでも買って帰ります。

Saikin zutto isogashiku shiteiru kara, tama niwa nyōbō no goma sutte, kēki demo katte kaerimasu.

Ⓑ 喜ぶよ、きっと。

Yorokobu yo, kitto.

Ⓐ I've always been so busy lately, so maybe I should butter up my wife for a change and bring home a cake.

Ⓑ I'm sure she'll be happy.

★ *nyōbo* = my wife

2 Ⓐ 部長はけっこうイケメンだし、面白いし、昔からモテたんじゃないですか。

Buchō wa kekkō ikemen da shi, omoshiroi shi, mukashi kara moteta n ja nai desu ka?

Ⓑ そんなふうにゴマすったって、おごらないよ。

Sonna fū ni gomasutta tte, ogoranai yo.

Ⓐ Boss, you're really handsome and funny. I bet you've always been popular with the ladies.

Ⓑ You can butter me up all you like, but I'm not paying for these drinks.

★ *ikemen* = good-looking

★ *moteru* = popular with girls, popular among the boys

★ *ogoru* = treat (someone), be on me

50

32 サバを読む
Saba o yomu

Fudge the numbers

In particular, to manipulate numbers. This comes from the idea of quickly and inaccurately counting mackerels at a fish market to sell them, as they are quick to lose their freshness.

1 Ⓐ さっき彼に年いくつって聞かれて、25歳ってサバ読んじゃった！

Sakki kare ni toshi ikutsu tte kikarete, nijū-go-sai tte saba yonjatta!

Ⓑ えーっ、ちょっとそれ、サバ読みすぎじゃない？

Ētt, chotto sore, saba yomisugi ja nai?

Ⓐ He just asked me how old I was, and I fudged the numbers and said 25!

Ⓑ Umm, really? Aren't you fudging them a little too much?

★ **sakki** = just now
★ **~sugiru** = ~ too much

2 Ⓐ 親にテキスト代もらった？

Oya ni tekisuto-dai moratta?

Ⓑ うん。サバ読んで2千円多くもらっちゃった。

Un. Saba yonde ni-sen-en ōku moracchatta.

Ⓐ Did you get money for your textbooks from your parents?

Ⓑ Yes. I fudged the numbers and got 2,000 yen extra.

★ **tekisuto-dai** = textbook fee

ぶつかる to bump (into)
Useful One-word Expressions in Japanese **9**

To have a difference of opinion with someone

Ex.) ときどき、彼と意見がぶつかる。
かれ　いけん
Sometimes, I have a clash of opinion with him.

33 手を抜く
Te o nuku

Cut corners

To omit necessary labor and do a careless job. Used when criticizing someone or being humble about oneself.

Listen & Speak

1 Ⓐ そんなに徹夜ばかりしないで、少しは手を抜くこと考えたら？

Sonna ni tesuya bakari shinaide, sukoshi wa te o nuku koto kangaetara?

Ⓑ そうは行かないよ。ちゃんとやらなきゃ。

Sō wa ikanai yo. Chanto yaranakya.

Ⓐ Why don't you consider cutting a few corners instead of doing so many all-nighters?

Ⓑ I can't do that. This needs to be done properly.

- ★ **tetsuya suru** = sit up all night
- ★ **~ bakari suru** = always ~
- ★ **chanto** = properly, surely

---

2 Ⓐ これ、おいしい！

Kore, oishī!

Ⓑ そう？　時間なかったから手抜いて作ったんだけど、おいしいならよかった。

Sō? Jikan nakatta kara te nuite tsukutta n da kedo, oishī nara yokatta.

Ⓐ This is delicious!

Ⓑ Really? I cut some corners because I didn't have time, but I'm glad it turned out to be tasty.

- ★ **jikan ga nai** = do not have time

34 お茶をにごす
ちゃ

O-cha o nigosu

Give an evasive reply

To gloss over an error for the time being in order to dodge the heart of the matter. Comes from the idea of someone who is not familiar with the tea ceremony making tea that simply looks appropriately cloudy before serving it.

Listen & Speak

1 Ⓐ夏のボーナスどうなるか、部長に聞いてみた？
なつ　　　　　　　　　ぶちょう　き

Natsu no bōnasu dō naru ka, buchō ni kīte mita?

Ⓐうん。でも、<u>お茶をにごされちゃって</u>、よくわからなかった。
ちゃ

Un. Demo, o-cha o nigosarechatte, yoku wakaranakatta.

Ⓐ Did you ask the boss what's happening with our summer bonuses?

Ⓑ Yes, but he gave an evasive reply and I wasn't really sure.

★ *bōnasu* = bonus

2 Ⓐ本当はどうなのって、しつこく聞かれたけど、うまく<u>お茶</u>
ほんとう　　　　　　　　　　　　き　　　　　　　　　　ちゃ
<u>をにごして</u>おいたよ。

Hontō wa dō na no tte, shitsukoku kikareta kedo, umaku o-cha o nigoshite oita yo.

Ⓑありがとう。助かった。
たす

Arigatō. Tasukatta.

Ⓐ She insistently asked me what the truth was, but I was able to give her an evasive reply.

Ⓑ Thanks. You helped me out.

★ *shitsukoku* = persistently
★ *tasukaru* = be helped

35 # 見て見ぬふりをする **Turn a blind eye**
Mite minu furi o suru

To pretend to not see or know about something despite actually having seen it or knowing about it.

1 Ⓐ どうしたの？ 30分も遅れて。

Dō shita no? Sanjuppun mo okurete.

Ⓑ ごめん。同僚がパソコンの調子が悪いっていうから、<u>見て見ぬふり</u>できなくて。

Gomen. Dōryō ga pasokon no chōshi ga warui tte yū kara, mite minu furi dekinakute.

Ⓐ What's the matter? You were thirty minutes late.

Ⓑ Sorry. My coworker said that his computer was acting up, and I couldn't turn a blind eye to the situation.

★ ***dōryō*** = colleague

---

2 Ⓐ 都会は嫌い。困っている人がいても<u>見て見ぬふりする</u>人多いから。

Tokai wa kirai. Komatteiru hito ga ite mo mite minu furi suru hito ōi kara.

Ⓑ そうかなあ。

Sō ka nā.

Ⓐ I don't like cities. Even when people need help, many people turn a blind eye.

Ⓑ I wonder.

★ ***tokai*** = city (⇔ country)

---

36 口先だけ
<ruby>口先<rt>く ち さき</rt></ruby>
Kuchisaki dake

Lip service; all take and no action

Casual words that do not have heart or emotion behind them, or words that are not accompanied with action.

1 Ⓐ 彼、資料集め手伝ってくれるって。
<ruby>彼<rt>かれ</rt></ruby>、<ruby>資料集<rt>し りょうあつ</rt></ruby>め<ruby>手伝<rt>て つだ</rt></ruby>

Kare, shiryō-atsume tesudatte kureru tte.

Ⓑ えっ、ほんと？　でも、あまり信用できないな。彼はいつも口先だけだから。
<ruby>信用<rt>しんよう</rt></ruby> <ruby>彼<rt>かれ</rt></ruby> <ruby>口先<rt>くちさき</rt></ruby>

Ett, honto? Demo, amari shin'yō dekinai na. Kare wa itsumo kuchisaki dake da kara.

Ⓐ He said he'd help gather materials.
Ⓑ What, really? I can't really trust him, though. He's always giving lip service.

★ **shiryō** = materials, documents (for something)
★ **shin'yō suru** = trust (someone)

2 みんな口先だけ。最初は大賛成とか、ぜひやりたいとか言ってたのに、結局誰もやらない。
<ruby>口先<rt>くちさき</rt></ruby> <ruby>最初<rt>さいしょ</rt></ruby> <ruby>大賛成<rt>だいさんせい</rt></ruby> <ruby>言<rt>い</rt></ruby> <ruby>結局誰<rt>けっきょくだれ</rt></ruby>

Minna kuchisaki dake. Saisho wa dai-sansē toka, zehi yaritai toka itteta noni, kekkyoku dare mo yaranai.

Everyone always gives nothing but lip service. They're in complete agreement at first, or they say they absolutely want to do it, but no one does it in the end.

★ **dai sansē** = be all for ~

Ⓐ When things are going well, fortunately

Ⓑ Efficient things: doing things efficiently

Ⓒ To have a strong interest, to become serious

Ⓓ Knowing the truth, understanding the situation

Ⓔ To not be bothered, to not be worried, to feel relieved

Ⓕ Doing something kindly, thoroughly, gently, and steadily

Ⓖ To strongly desire, to crave

Ⓗ Dodging something so that it is more convenient for you

Ⓘ To influence

37 口説く
くどく
Kudoku

To woo; to make a move on; to lure

To enthusiastically explain so that the listener's feelings are in line with your intentions. To passionately convince someone of the opposite sex to have an interest in you. Comes from the expression 「くどくど言う」 (to say persistently).

Listen & Speak

1 Ⓐ 田中さんを口説いて、司会をしてもらいましょうよ。

Tanaka-san o kudoite, shikai o shite moraimashō yo.

Ⓑ そうだね。田中さんならピッタリだもの。

Sō da ne. Tanaka-san nara pittari da mono.

Ⓐ We should lure Tanaka-san into being the moderator.

Ⓑ Yes, he would be perfect for the role.

★ *shikai* = master of ceremony, emcee

★ *~ni pittari* = suit for ~, perfect for ~

2 Ⓐ 〈映画を見ながら〉

一度でいいから、あんなふうに口説かれてみたい。
〈Ēga o minagara〉

Ichi-do de ī kara, anna fū ni kudokarete mitai.

Ⓑ 私も。

Watashi mo.

Ⓐ (While watching a movie) Just once, I wish someone would woo me like that.

Ⓑ Me too.

★ *anna fū ni* = I ike that, that way

38 一か八か
いち ばち
Ichi ka bachi ka

Take one's chances

To daringly do something despite having no guarantee that it will go well. Comes from a gambling term, where a game is played that decides winners based on whether the sum of two two dice comes up even (丁) or odd (半). The top of the 「丁」 kanji is 「一」, while the top of the 「半」 kanji is 「八」.
ちょう   はん   ちょう   いち
はん   はち

Listen & Speak

1 Ⓐ 作品、1位に選ばれたね。おめでとう！
さくひん い えら
Sakuhin, ichi-i ni erabareta ne. Omedetō!

Ⓑ ありがとう。自信なかったけど、一か八かで応募してよかったよ。
じしん いち ばち おうぼ
Arigatō. Jishin nakatta kedo, ichi ka bachi ka de ōbo shite yokatta yo.

Ⓐ Your work was given first prize. Congratulations!
Ⓑ Thank you. I wasn't confident, but I'm glad I took my chances and applied.

★ *sakuhin* = work
★ *ōbo suru* = apply for

2 Ⓐ 一か八か試合に出てみない？
いち ばち しあい で
Ichi ka bachi ka shiai ni dete minai?

Ⓑ えーっ、無理だよ。練習、全然足りないよ。
むり れんしゅう ぜんぜん た
Ētt, muri da yo. Renshū, zen-zen tarinai yo.

Ⓐ Do you want to take your chances and participate in the match?
Ⓑ What? There's no way. I haven't practiced nearly enough.

★ *muri(na)* = impossible, unreasonable
★ *~ga tarinai* = lack ~, be short of ~

Ⓐ When things are going well / fortunately

Ⓑ Efficient things, doing things efficiently

Ⓒ To have a strong interest, to become serious

Ⓓ Knowing the truth, understanding the situation

Ⓔ To not be bothered / to not be worried, to feel relieved

Ⓕ Doing something kindly, thoroughly, gently, and steadily

Ⓖ To strongly desire, to crave

Ⓗ Dodging something to that it is more convenient for you

Ⓘ To influence

39 頑張り屋
がんばや
Ganbari-ya

Tenacious

Someone who gives unsparing effort to anything they do, tackling things with everything they have. Used as praise by a superior to someone below them, or among extremely close individuals.

Listen & Speak

1 Ⓐ へー、働きながら大学に通ってるんだ。頑張り屋だなあ。
はたら　　　　　　だいがく　　かよ　　　　　がんばや

Hē hatarakinagara daigaku ni kayotteru n da. Ganbari-ya da nā.

Ⓑ そんなことないですよ。

Sonna koto nai desu yo.

> Ⓐ Wow, you're working while also going to university? You're so tenacious.
> Ⓑ Not at all.

★ **kayou** = go to

2 Ⓐ 彼女一人に任せて大丈夫かなあ。
かのじょひとり　まか　　だいじょうぶ

Kanojo hitori ni makasete daijōbu ka nā.

Ⓑ 大丈夫だよ。ああ見えて、けっこう頑張り屋だから。
だいじょうぶ　　　　み　　　　　　　　　がんばや

Daijōbu da yo. Ā miete, kekkō ganbari-ya da kara.

> Ⓐ I wonder if I can leave it all up to her.
> Ⓑ It's fine. She's pretty tenacious, despite how she may look.

★ **~ni makaseru** = leave something to ~, trust ~

★ **ā miete ~** = may not look it, but ~

彼 he
かれ

Useful One-word Expressions in Japanese

a boyfriend ＊ Also "*kareshi*"

Ex.) 彼を両親に会わせる／今は彼氏はいません。
かれ　りょうしん　あ　　　　　いま　かれし

I will introduce my boyfriend to my parents./ I don't have a boyfriend at the moment.

40 頭が切れる
あたま き
Atama ga kireru

Sharp-minded

Someone who has a clear and sharp mind that works quickly. Used as praise.

1 Ⓐ さすが、佐藤さん、説得力ある！
さとう せっとくりょく
Sasuga, Satō-san, settoku-ryoku aru!

Ⓑ 頭、切れるよね。誰も反論できなかったもんね。
あたま き だれ はんろん
Atama, kireru yo ne. Dare mo hanron dekinakatta mon ne.

Ⓐ You can always count on Satou-san to be persuasive!

Ⓑ She's sharp-minded. No one was able to object to her.

★ **settokuryoku ga aru** = persuasive, convincing

★ **hanron suru** = offer a counterargument, refute

2 Ⓐ うらやましいなあ。美人だし、頭も切れるし。
びじん あたま き
Urayamashīnā. Bijin da shi, atama mo kireru shi.

Ⓑ ほんと。彼女だったら、どこでも就職できそう。
かのじょ しゅうしょく
Honto. Kanojo dattara, doko demo shūshoku dekisō.

Ⓐ I'm so jealous. She's beautiful and she's sharp-minded.

Ⓑ Yes. It seems like she'd be able to get hired anywhere.

★ **urayamashī** = be jealous, envy someone

★ **shūshoku suru** = find employment

彼女 she
かのじょ

Useful One-word Expressions in Japanese 11

A girlfriend

Ex.) 僕の彼女を紹介します。／今、彼女はいません。
ぼく かのじょ しょうかい いま かのじょ
I'll introduce my girlfriend. / I don't have a girlfriend now.

41 人気者
にんきもの
Ninki-mono

Popular (person)

Someone who is popular with those around them and is liked by all. Used as praise.

1 Ⓐ あの子、オリンピックでメダル取ってから、急に人気者になったね。

Ano ko, orinpikku de medaru totte kara, kyū ni ninki-mono ni natta ne.

Ⓑ そうだね、かわいいし、嫌いな人いないんじゃないかな。

Sō da ne. Kawaī shi, kiraina hito inai n ja nai ka na.

Ⓐ She suddenly became popular after getting that medal in the Olympics.

Ⓑ You're right. She's cute, and I doubt there's anyone who dislikes her.

★ ***medaru*** = medal

2 Ⓐ ごめん、もう行かないと。別の約束があるの。

Gomen, mō ikanai to. Betsu no yakusoku ga aru no.

Ⓑ そう……。人気者はつらいね。また、時間あるときに来て。

Sō .... Ninki-mono wa tsurai ne. Mata, jikan aru toki ni kite.

Ⓐ Sorry, I need to go. I have another appointment.

Ⓑ Oh... It must be hard being popular. Come back again when you have time.

★ ***yakusoku*** = promise, appointment

★ ***tsurai*** = hard, harsh, tough, trying

42 おっちょこちょい
Occhokochoi
Scatterbrained

Someone who does not think calmly and often acts rashly. 「おっ」 is an interjection used when surprised, while「ちょこ」is from「ちょこちょこ」, used to describe small movements, and 「ちょい」 means "a little bit." This term comes from a combination of all three. Used with some degree of affection to gently rein someone in or to be modest about yourself.

J Assessing people, describing people as a certain type

K To be busy or flustered while acting

L To be nervous, to be worried

M Differences

N Encouraging someone

O Dealing with a situation, dealing with a situation gently

P Taking criticism, blame, or an attack

Q Arrogant, proud, or stubborn attitudes

R To not match, to become weary, to be fed up

1 Ⓐ わっ、ごめん！ コーヒーこぼしちゃった！

Watt, gomen! Kōhī koboshichatta!

Ⓑ もう。ほんとにおっちょこちょいなんだから。気をつけて。
き

Mō. Honto ni occhokochoi na n da kara. Ki o tsukete.

Ⓐ Agh, sorry! I spilled your coffee!

Ⓑ Oh, you're so scatterbrained. Be careful.

★ **kobosu** = spill

2 Ⓐ 山下さんって、おっちょこちょいかなあ。見て、このハガ
やました み
キ。切手が逆さになってる。
きって さか

Yamashita-san tte, occhokochoi ka nā. Mite, kono hagaki. Kitte ga sakasa ni natteru.

Ⓑ ほんとだ。

Honto da.

Ⓐ I wonder if Yamashita-san could be scatterbrained. Just look at this postcard. The stamp is upside-down.

Ⓑ You're right.

★ **sakasa** = upside down

43 腰が低い
こし　ひく
Koshi ga hikui

Humble

Someone who is modest, does not intrude, and acts more reserved than others. Used as praise.

1 Ⓐ 小池さんて、どんな人？　来週初めて会うんだけど。
こいけ　　　　　　　　　　ひと　　らいしゅうはじ　　　あ

Koike-san te, donna hito? Raishū hajimete au n da kedo.

Ⓑ いい人ですよ。<u>腰が低くて</u>、いつも人より先に挨拶して、
ひと　　　　　　こし　ひく　　　　　　　ひと　　さき　あいさつ
深く頭を下げるような人です。
ふか　あたま　さ　　　　　　ひと

Ī hito desu yo. Koshi ga hikukute, itsumo hito yori saki ni aisatsu shite, fukaku atama o sageru yō na hito desu.

Ⓐ What kind of person is Koike-san? I'm meeting him for the first time next week.

Ⓑ He's a good person. He's humble, and he's the kind to always be the first to greet others and bow deeper than them.

★ ***atama o sageru*** = bow

2 Ⓐ 課長はすごく仕事ができる人なのに、いつも<u>腰が低い</u>ね。
か　ちょう　　　　　　しごと　　　　　　ひと　　　　　　　　こし　ひく

Kachō wa sugoku shigoto ga dekiru hito na noni, itsumo koshi ga hikui ne.

Ⓑ そうそう。だから部下に好かれるんだよね。
ぶ　か　す

Sōsō. Dakara buka ni sukareru n da yo ne.

Ⓐ The section chief is so good at his job, but he's always humble.

Ⓑ Yes, it's why his subordinates like him so much.

★ ***buka*** = subordinate
★ ***sukareru*** = be liked

44 口が堅い
くち かた
Kuchi ga katai

Tight-lipped

Someone who properly keeps secrets they've heard from others, never revealing them. Used as praise.

Listen & Speak

1 Ⓐどんな人が秘書に向いてると思いますか。
ひと ひしょ む おも
Donna hito ga hisho ni muiteru to omoimasu ka?

Ⓑ気のつく人ですね、あと、口の堅い人。
き ひと くち かた ひと
Ki no tsuku hito desu ne. Ato, kuchi no katai hito.

Ⓐ What kind of person do you think would make a good secretary?

Ⓑ Someone who is careful, and also tight-lipped.

★ **(yoku) ki ga/no tsuku** = be quick of perception, attentive

2 Ⓐどうしよう。水野さんに聞いてみようかなあ。
みず の き
Dō shiyō. Mizuno-san ni kīte miyō ka nā.

Ⓑいいと思うよ。彼女は口堅いし。
おも かのじょ くちかた
Ī to omou yo. Kanojo wa kuchi katai shi.

Ⓐ What should I do? Maybe I should try asking Mizuno-san.

Ⓑ I think that's a good idea. She's tight-lipped, too.

★ **dō shiyō** = What should I do? / What can I do?

体 body
からだ

Useful One-word Expressions in Japanese 12

Health and physical strength

Ex.) 体に気をつけてください。／体をこわす／体が持たない。
からだ き からだ からだ も
Please take care of your health. / To ruin one's health/ To run out of energy .

J Assessing people, describing people as a certain type

K To be busy or flustered while acting

L To be nervous, to be worried

M Differences

N Encouraging someone

O Dealing with a situation sternly, dealing with a situation gently

P Taking criticism, blame, or an attack

Q Arrogant, proud, or stubborn attitudes

R To not match, to become weary, to be fed up

45 一匹狼
Ippiki-ōkami
(いっぴきおおかみ)

Lone wolf

Someone who acts alone and independently, rather than joining groups and aligning themselves with others. Someone who prefers to be alone rather than acting or working in a group. A metaphor comparing someone to a wolf who leaves its pack and acts alone.

Listen & Speak

1 Ⓐ 勉強会に田中さんも誘ってみる？
Benkyō-kai ni Tanaka-san mo sasotte miru?

Ⓑ そうだね……。でも、彼は一匹狼だから、誘っても来ないんじゃない？
So da ne.... Demo, kare wa ippiki-ōkami da kara, sasotte mo konai n ja nai?

Ⓐ Do you want to try inviting Tanaka-san to the study session, too?

Ⓑ You have a point... But he is a lone wolf, so don't you think he wouldn't come even if we invited him?

★ **sasou** = invite someone

2 Ⓐ 彼はいつも一人でいるね。
Kare wa itsumo hitori de iru ne.

Ⓑ 一匹狼だからね。でも、話すと面白い人だよ。
Ippiki-ōkami da kara ne. Demo, hanasu to omoshiroi hito da yo.

Ⓐ He's always alone.

Ⓑ That's because he's a lone wolf. He's interesting if you talk to him, though.

★ **omoshiroi hito** = interesting person

46 寂しがり屋
さ び や

Attention-hungry;
get lonely easily

Sabishigari-ya

Someone who likes being with others and receiving attention while disliking being alone.

1 Ⓐ また、妹さんから電話？
いもうと でんわ

Mata, imōto-san kara denwa?

Ⓑ そう。寂しがり屋で、しょっちゅう電話してくるの。
さ び や でん わ

Sō. Sabishigari-ya de, shocchū denwa shite kuru no.

Ⓐ Another phone call from your little sister?

Ⓑ Yes. She's attention-hungry, so she calls me all the time.

★ **shocchū** = always, frequently

2 Ⓐ あんなふうに言ってるけど、彼も本当は寂しがり屋なんです。
い かれ ほんとう さ び や

Anna fū ni itteru kedo, kare mo hontō wa sabishigari-ya na n desu.

Ⓑ そうなんですか。

Sō na n desu ka.

Ⓐ He says things like that, but he's actually attention-hungry.

Ⓑ Is that so?

★ **anna fū ni** = like that, that way

頭 head
あたま

Useful One-word Expressions in Japanese 13

I. The function of the brain, the ability to think   2. The first part

Ex.1) 頭がいい・悪い／頭の回転が早い
あたま あたま かいてん はや
Clever, unintelligent / quick thinking

Ex.2) ４月の頭／曲の頭
がつ あたま きょく あたま
The beginning of April / the beginning of a piece of music

Ⓙ Assessing people, describing people as a certain type

Ⓚ To be busy or flustered while acting

Ⓛ To be nervous, to be worried

Ⓜ Differences

Ⓝ Encouraging someone

Ⓞ Dealing with a situation sternly, dealing with a situation gently

Ⓟ Taking criticism, blame, or an attack

Ⓠ Arrogant, proud, or stubborn attitudes

Ⓡ To not match, to become weary, to be fed up

47 負けず嫌い
ま　　ぎら
Makezu-girai

Sore loser

Someone who dislikes losing and wants to be superior to others.
More often used as a negative evaluation than a positive one.

1 Ⓐ彼は負けず嫌いだから、スポーツ選手に向いてるよね。
かれ　　ま　ぎら　　　　　　　　　　　　せんしゅ　む

Kare wa makezu-girai da kara, supōtsu-senshu ni muiteru yo ne.

Ⓑそうだね。負けると本当に悔しそうだものね。
ま　　　　ほんとう　くや

Sō da ne. Makeru to hontō ni kuyashisō da mono ne.

Ⓐ He's a sore loser, which would make him a good athlete.

Ⓑ You're right. He really does seem frustrated when he loses.

★ **~ni muiteiru**=be suited for~, be cut out for ~

★ **makeru** = lose (a game), be beaten

★ **kuyashī** = be frustrated, be mortified

2 Ⓐ人から批判されるの、大嫌いでしょ？
ひと　　ひはん　　　　　だいきら

Hito kara hihan sareru no, daikirai desho?

Ⓑまあ、そうかな。負けず嫌いだからね。
ま　ぎら

Mā, sō ka na. Makezu-girai da kara ne.

Ⓐ Don't you hate being criticized by people?

Ⓑ Well, yes. I am a sore loser.

★ **hihan suru** = criticize

48 恥ずかしがり屋 Shy
は や

Hazukashigari-ya

Someone who is bashful, shy, and easily embarrassed over anything.

1 Ⓐ いやです。人前でそんなことするの、恥ずかしいです。
ひとまえ は

Iya desu. Hitomae de sonna koto suruno, hazukashī desu.

Ⓑ だめだよ、そんな<u>恥ずかしがり屋</u>では。勇気を出して、やっ
は や ゆうき だ
てみてごらん。

Dame da yo, sonna hazukashigari-ya de wa. Yūki o dashite,
yatte mite goran.

Ⓐ No, it'd be embarrassing to do
something like that in front of other
people.

Ⓑ You can't be so shy. Be brave and
give it a try.

★ *hitomae de* = in public, in
front of people

★ *yūki o dasu* = muster up one's
courage

2 Ⓐ 彼女は<u>恥ずかしがり屋</u>だから、自分から人に話しかけるこ
かのじょ は や じ ぶん ひと はな
とができないみたいね。

Kanojo wa hazukashigari-ya da kara, jibun kara hito ni
hanashikakeru koto ga dekinai mitai ne.

Ⓑ そうだね。もう少し積極的だといいんだけど。
すこ せっきょくてき

Sō da ne. Mō sukoshi sekkyokuteki da to ī n da kedo.

Ⓐ She's shy, so she doesn't seem to
be able to start a conversation with
others.

Ⓑ Yes, I wish she could be a little more
assertive.

★ *(jibun kara) hanashikakeru*
= start to talk to someone

★ *sekkyokuteki (na)* = positive

49 泣き虫
なき むし
Nakimushi

Crybaby

Someone who cries over everything.

Listen & Speak

1 Ⓐ こんなにしてくださるなんて感激です[泣く]！
かんげき　　　な

Konna ni shite kudasaru nante kangeki dasu [naku]!

Ⓑ 泣き虫だなあ。そんなに泣かなくてもいいのに。
な　むし　　　　　　　　　　な

Nakimushi da nā. Sonna ni nakanakute mo ī no ni.

Ⓐ I'm so moved that you'd do all of this for me! [cries]

Ⓑ You're such a crybaby. You don't need to cry so much.

★ **kangeki** = be moved

2 Ⓐ 彼女、本当に泣き虫で、テレビ見ながら毎日泣くんです。
かのじょ　ほんとう　な　むし　　　　　　み　　　　　まいにち な

Kanojo, hontō ni nakimushi de, terebi minagara mainichi naku n desu.

Ⓑ へえ、そうなんだ。まあ、怒るよりいいんじゃない？
おこ

Hē, sō nanda. Mā, okoru yori ī n ja nai?

Ⓐ She's such a crybaby. She cries while watching television every day.

Ⓑ Wow, really? Well, isn't it better than getting mad?

★ **okoru** = get angry

50 気分屋
（き ぶん や）
Kibun-ya

Moody

Someone whose mood constantly changes. Their mood may sour just as soon as they seem like they are in a good mood. Often used as a negative assessment.

1 Ⓐ うちのボスは気分屋だから、すごく疲れる。
Uchi no bosu wa kibun-ya da kara, sugoku tsukareru.

Ⓑ わかる、わかる。気分屋って困るよね。
Wakaru, wakaru. Kibun-ya tte komaru yo ne.

- Ⓐ Our boss is so moody that it's exhausting.
- Ⓑ I know how it is. Moody people are such a bother, aren't they.

★ ***bosu*** = boss

2 Ⓐ あの人、明るく挨拶してくれる時とこっちが挨拶しても無視する時と差が激しい。
Ano hito, akaruku aisatsu shite kureru toki to kocchi ga aisatsu shite mo mushi suru toki to sa ga hageshī.

Ⓑ 確かに。気分屋なんだろうね。
Tashikani. Kibun-ya nandarō ne.

- Ⓐ That person can be so different in the way he acts. Sometimes he'll cheerfully greet me, but other times he'll ignore my greetings.
- Ⓑ That's for sure. He must be a moody person.

★ ***mushi suru*** = ignore
★ ***sa*** = difference
★ ***hageshī*** = extreme

J Assessing people, describing people as a certain type

K To be busy or flustered while acting

L To be nervous, to be worried

M Differences

N Encouraging someone

O Dealing with a situation sternly, dealing with a situation gently

P Taking criticism, blame, or an attack

Q Arrogant, proud, or stubborn attitudes

R To not match, to become weary, to be fed up

51 甘えん坊
あま　　ぼう
Amaenbō

Spoilt; spoiled child

Someone who is very dependent and tries to takes advantage of others' kindness.

Listen & Speak

1 Ⓐ 彼女は三人兄弟の一番下だって。
かのじょ　さんにんきょうだい　いちばんした
Kaojo wa san-nin kyōdai no ichiban shita da tte.

Ⓑ やっぱり。甘えん坊だものね。
あま　ぼう
Yappari. Amaenbō da mono ne.

Ⓐ I hear she's the youngest of three siblings.
Ⓑ That makes sense. She's so spoilt.

★ ***ichiban shita*** = youngest

2 Ⓐ 一人じゃ心配だから、一緒に行ってくれない？
ひとり　しんぱい　いっしょ　い
Hitori ja shinpai da kara, issho ni itte kurenai?

Ⓑ 甘えん坊だなあ。
あま　ぼう
Amaenbō da nā.

Ⓐ I'm worried about going alone. Could you come with me?
Ⓑ You're so spoilt.

★ ***shinpai*** = be worried, be uneasy

明るい bright
あか

Useful One-word Expressions in Japanese 14

1. Personality, atmosphere, having a cheerful expression
2. Having hope and joy
3. "Being knowledgeable about ..." "being well-informed about ..."

Ex.1) 明るい人／明るい声／明るいニュース
あか　ひと　あか　こえ　あか
A cheerful person / a cheerful voice / happy news

Ex.2) 明るい気持ち
あか　きも
Happy feeling

Ex.3) 経済に明るい
けいざい　あか
Well-informed about economics

52 お人好し
ひと よ
ohitoyoshi

Softhearted

Someone who acts immediately without any thought to how it may help or harm themselves. Someone who sees everything as well-intentioned, quickly believes others, and is easily fooled. Often used to gently rein someone in or as a mild negative assessment.

1 Ⓐ土曜日、引っ越しの手伝いがあるから僕は行けないなあ。
どようび ひ こ てつだ ぼく い
Doyōbi, hikkoshi no tetsudai ga aru kara boku wa ikenai nā.

Ⓑまた？　お人好しなんだから。
ひと よ
Mata? Ohitoyoshi na n da kara.

Ⓐ I don't think I can go, I have to help someone move on Saturday.

Ⓑ Again? You're so softhearted.

★ ***tanomareru*** = be asked to do something

2 Ⓐ兄はお人好しで、頼まれたらいやと言えないんですよ。
あに ひと よ たの い
Ani wa ohitoyoshi de, tanomaretara iya to ienai n desu yo.

Ⓑ私の父もです。困りますよね。
わたし ちち こま
Watashi no chichi mo desu. Komarimasu yo ne.

Ⓐ My older brother is softhearted, so he can't say no to a request.

Ⓑ My father, too. It's bothersome, isn't it?

★ ***tanomu*** = ask, request, beg

暗い dark
くら

Useful One-word Expressions in Japanese 15

1. Personality, expression, a gloomy atmosphere, a feeling of melancholy
2. Having no hope or joy

Ex.1) 暗い人／暗い顔／暗い歌／暗いニュース
くら ひと くら かお くら うた くら
A gloomy person / a gloomy expression / a depressing song / depressing news

Ex.2) 暗い気持ち／暗い将来
くら きも くら しょうらい
A feeling of depression / a bleak future

Listen & Speak

J Assessing people, describing people as a certain type

K To be busy or flustered while acting

L To be nervous, to be worried

M Differences

N Encouraging someone

O Dealing with a situation sternly, dealing with a situation gently

P Taking criticism, blame, or an attack

Q Arrogant, proud, or stubborn attitudes

R To not match, to become weary, to be fed up

53 おしゃべり

Oshaberi

Loose lips; chatterbox

To speak a lot when talking casually to a friend, to easily reveal secrets, or to be someone who has such tendencies. Used as a negative assessment. Also used as a na-adjective, such as 「おしゃべりな」.

Listen & Speak

1 ❶このこと、彼には内緒にしておこう。おしゃべりだから。

Kono koto, kare ni wa naisho ni shite okō. Oshaberi da kara.

❷そうだね。そのほうが安全だね。

Sō da ne. Sono hō ga anzen da ne.

---

❶ Let's keep this a secret from him. He has loose lips.

❷ You're right. It'll be safer that way.

★ **naisho ni suru** = keep something secret

★ **anzen (na)** = safe

---

2 ❶君ら二人ともおしゃべりだから、会話が止まらないんじゃない？

Kimira futari tomo oshaberi da kara, kaiwa ga tomaranai n ja nai?

❷そう。昨日も電話で 1 時間しゃべっちゃった。

Sō. Kinō mo denwa de ichi-jikan shabecchatta.

---

❶ You two are chatterboxes, so your conversations must never stop.

❷ You're right. We talked on the phone yesterday for an hour.

★ **~tomo** = both of ~, all of ~

---

54 ノリがいい・悪い
_{わる}

Gets into the mood / Doesn't get into the mood

Nori ga ī / warui

「ノリがいい」 describes someone who is able to match their mood to an excited situation and act appropriately. On the other hand someone who cannot match their mood to an excited situation and stays uninterested is described as 「ノリが悪い」.
_{わる}

J Assessing people, describing people as a certain type

K To be busy or flustered while acting

L To be nervous, to be worried

M Differences

N Encouraging someone

O Dealing with a situation sternly, dealing with a situation gently

P Taking criticism, blame, or an attack

Q Arrogant, proud or stubborn attitudes

R To not match, to become weary, to be fed up

Listen & Speak

1 **Ⓐ** 昨日のボーリング大会、盛り上がったね。
_{きのう たいかい も あ}

Kinō no bōringu taikai, moriagatta ne.

Ⓑ うん。<u>ノリがいい</u>メンバーばかりだったからね。

Un. Nori ga ī menbā bakari datta kara ne.

Ⓐ People really got into yesterday's bowling tournament, didn't they?

Ⓑ Yes. It's because it was full of people who can get into the mood.

★ *moriagaru* = get lively, get into swing

2 **Ⓐ** 一人だけ踊らないで、ずっと飲んでたね。
_{ひとり おど の}

Hitori dake odoranai de, zutto nondeta ne.

Ⓑ いつもそう。彼は<u>ノリが悪い</u>から。
_{かれ わる}

Itsumo sō. Kare wa nori ga warui kara.

Ⓐ He was the one person not dancing. He just drank the whole time.

Ⓑ He's always like that. He doesn't get into the mood.

★ *zutto* = all the time, whole time

55 お調子者
ちょうしもの
Ochōshi-mono

Frivolous; easily flatterd

Someone who keeps in step with others, is easily flattered, and is full of themselves. Also used to describe someone who casually keeps in step with others without accepting responsibility for their words. Often used in a negative way.

1 Ⓐ 田口さんがいい方法があるから大丈夫だって言ってたよ。
Taguchi-san ga ī hōhō ga aru kara daijōbu da tte itteta yo.

Ⓑ ほんとかなあ。彼は<u>お調子者</u>だからね。あまり期待しないほうがいいと思うよ。
Honto ka nā. Kare wa ochōshi-mono da kara ne. Amari kitai shinai hō ga ī to omou yo.

Ⓐ Taguchi-san said it would be okay because there's a good way to do it.

Ⓑ I wonder if that's true. He's a frivolous person, so you shouldn't count on him too much.

★ *kitai suru* = expect

2 Ⓐ みんなが歌え歌えって言うから、2曲も歌っちゃったよ。
Minna ga utae utae tte yū kara, ni-kyoku mo utacchatta yo.

Ⓑ そうなの!? <u>お調子者</u>なんだから。
Sō na no!? Ochōshi-mono na n da kara.

Ⓐ Everyone said to sing, so I ended up singing two songs.

Ⓑ You're so frivolous.

★ *utau* = sing (a song)

56 ひねくれ者
<small>もの</small>
Hinekure-mono

Contrarian; contrary person

Someone who is unable to take things in a frank way and takes them in a contrarian fashion. Often used in a negative way.

1 Ⓐもう少し相手の話をよく聞いたほうがいいんじゃない？
<small>すこ あいて はなし き</small>

Mō sukoshi aite no hanashi o yoku kīta hō ga ī n ja nai?

Ⓑすいませんね。どうせ僕は<u>ひねくれ者</u>ですから。
<small>ぼく もの</small>

Suimasen ne. Dōse boku wa hinekure-mono desu kara.

Ⓐ Shouldn't you listen a bit more to what others have to say?

Ⓑ I'm sorry. I'm just such a contrarian.

★ **suimasen** = a little crude way of saying "*sumimasen*"

---

2 Ⓐ石川さんって、<u>ひねくれ者</u>だよね。みんなで合格祝しようっ
<small>いしかわ もの ごうかくいわ</small>
て言ったら「誰でも合格できる試験だから必要ない」だって。
<small>い だれ ごうかく しけん ひつよう</small>

Ishikawa-san tte, hinekure-mono da yo ne. Minna de gōkaku-iwai shiyō tte ittara "dare demo gōkaku dekiru shiken da kara hitsuyō nai" da tte.

Ⓑまあ、そういう人だから。気にしない、気にしない。
<small>ひと き き</small>

Mā, sōyū hito da kara. Ki ni shinai, Ki ni shinai.

Ⓐ Ishikawa-san is a contrarian. Everyone said we should celebrate her passing the test, but she told me "There's no need because anyone could pass that test."

Ⓑ Well, that's the kind of person she is. Don't worry yourself over it.

★ **~iwai** = celebration on ~
★ **Ki ni shinai.** (⇐ **Ki ni shinaide kudasai.**) = Never mind. / Don't worry.

Ⓙ Assessing people, describing people as a certain type

Ⓚ To be busy or flustered while acting

Ⓛ To be nervous, to be worried

Ⓜ Differences

Ⓝ Encouraging someone

Ⓞ Dealing with a situation sternly, dealing with a situation gently

Ⓟ Taking criticism, blame, or an attack

Ⓠ Arrogant, proud, or stubborn attitudes

Ⓡ To not match, to become weary, to be fed up

57 頭が固い
あたま かた
Atama ga katai

Stubborn

Someone who is not accommodating and cannot be flexible about things. Someone who thinks of things in an extremely serious and stiff way. Used in a negative way.

1 Ⓐ 山口さん、計画が変わるんだったら仕事を降りるって。
やまぐち けいかく か しごと お

Yamaguchi-san, kēkaku ga kawaru n dattara shigoto o oriru tte.

Ⓑ やっぱり。彼は頭固いからなあ。
かれ あたまかた

Yappari. Kare wa atama katai kara nā.

Ⓐ Yamaguchi-san said he would take himself off the job if the plan changes.

Ⓑ I thought that might happen. He's so stubborn.

★ **kēkaku** = plan, project
★ **~ o oriru** = quit ~

2 Ⓐ 広告の仕事は、頭の固い人は向かないと思う。
こうこく しごと あたま かた ひと む おも

Kōkoku no shigoto wa, atama no katai hito wa mukanai to omou.

Ⓑ そうだね。時代の変化を感じられる人でないとね。
じだい へんか かん ひと

Sō da ne. Jidai no henka o kanjirareru hito de nai to ne.

Ⓐ I don't think advertising is a good job for stubborn people.

Ⓑ You're right. You need to be someone who can feel how the times are changing.

★ **kōkoku** = advertisement
★ **jidai** = era, age, times

首 neck
くび

Useful One-word Expressions in Japanese 16

1. Part of the head   2. The neck of a garment   3. Dismissal from a job

Ex.1) 首を横に振る
くび よこ ふ
To shake one's head

Ex.2) Ｔシャツの首／丸首
くび まるくび
The neck of a T-shirt / a round neck

Ex.3) 彼は首になった。
かれ くび
He was fired.

58 頭が下がる
あたま さ
Atama ga sagaru

Take one's hat off to

Feelings of wanting to bow your head to someone out of admiration for their actions or attitude. Used in a positive way.

Listen & Speak

1 Ⓐ 遠くから災害ボランティアに来る人って、えらいね。
とお さいがい く ひと
Tōku kara saigai-boranthia ni kuru hito tte, erai ne.

Ⓑ ほんと。頭が下がるよね。
あたま さ
Honto. Atama ga sagaru yo ne.

Ⓐ Aren't people who travel from far away to volunteer at disaster sites so admirable?

Ⓑ You're very right. I want to take my hat off to them.

★ *saigai* = disaster
★ *boranthia* = volunteer

2 Ⓐ 由美さんには頭が下がるよ。仕事しながら義理のお父さん
ゆ み あたま さ しごと ぎり とう
の世話をして、お祭りの委員もやるなんて。
せ わ まつ い いん
Yumi-san niwa atama ga sagaru yo. Shigoto shinagara giri no otōsan no sewa o shite, o-matsuri no iin mo yaru nante.

Ⓑ いえ、そんなことないですよ。
Ie, sonna koto nai desu yo.

Ⓐ I want to take my hat off to you, Yumi-san. You're taking care of your father-in-law while working, and you're even on a festival committee.

Ⓑ No, not at all.

★ *giri no ~* = ~ in law
★ *iin* = member of the committee

J Assessing people, describing people as a certain type

K To be busy or flustered while acting

L To be nervous, to be worried

M Differences

N Encouraging someone

O Dealing with a situation sternly, dealing with a situation gently

P Taking criticism, blame, or an attack

Q Arrogant, proud, or stubborn attitudes

R To not match, to become weary, to be fed up

77

59 パニクる

To panic

Panikuru

A state of panicking after losing one's composure or becoming flustered due to a sudden occurrence.

Listen & Speak

1 Ⓐ 急に本社から社長が来るって聞いて、パニクっちゃった。
きゅう　ほんしゃ　しゃちょう　く　き

Kyū ni honsha kara shachō ga kuru tte kīte, panikucchatta.

Ⓑ 社長、怖いからね。
しゃちょう　こわ

Shachō, kowai kara ne.

Ⓐ I panicked after headquarters suddenly told me the president was coming.
Ⓑ Yeah, I'm afraid of the president.

★ **honsha** = head office

2 Ⓐ どうしたの？

Dō shita no?

Ⓑ ここに置いたはずの USB がなくて、さっきからパニクってるんです。
お

Koko ni oita hazu no yūesubī ga nakute, sakki kara panikutteru n desu.

Ⓐ What's the matter?
Ⓑ I've been panicking because I can't find the USB I thought I put down here.

★ **~shita hazu** = I thought that I did ~

J Assessing people, describing people as a certain type

K To be busy or flustered while acting

L To be nervous, to be worried

M Differences

N Encouraging someone

O Dealing with a situation sternly; dealing with a situation gently

P Taking criticism, blame, or an attack

Q Arrogant, proud, or stubborn attitudes

R To not match, to become weary, to be fed up

60 バタバタする
Batabata suru

Make a commotion; running around everywhere

To be extremely busy and not calm. Used to illustrate a bird making noise and flapping its wings around or a person moving around a room noisily.

1 Ⓐ すみません、ご連絡が遅くなってしまって。いろいろあってバタバタしてたものですから。

Sumimasen, go-renraku ga osoku natte shimatte. Iroiro atte batabata shiteta mono desu kara.

Ⓑ いえいえ、大変でしたね。

Ieie, taihen deshita ne.

Ⓐ I'm sorry that I took so long to contact you. I had a lot happening, and I was running around everywhere.

Ⓑ Not at all. That must have been tough.

★ *go-renraku* = contacting

2 Ⓐ 金曜の夜、映画を見に行かない？

Kin'yō no yoru, ēga o mi ni ikanai?

Ⓑ ごめん、今急ぎの仕事でバタバタしてて、余裕ないんだ。

Gomen, ima isogi no shigoto de batabata shitete, yoyū nai n da.

Ⓐ Would you like to go see a movie Friday night?

Ⓑ I'm sorry, I don't have time because I've been running around everywhere with an urgent job.

★ *isogi no* = urgent, rush
★ *yoyū* = margin, allowance

61 ぶっつけ本番

ほんばん

Buttsuke honban

Off the cuff; unrehearsed

To do something suddenly and without any preparation. An expression that draws a comparison to a stage performance taking place without any practice.

Listen & Speak

1 Ⓐ まだ一度もみんなで練習してないね。
いち ど　　　　　　　　　れんしゅう

Mada ichido mo minna de renshū shite nai ne.

Ⓑ うん。でも、しょうがないよ。ぶっつけ本番でやろう。
ほんばん

Un. Demo, shōganai yo. Buttsuke honban de yarō.

Ⓐ We haven't practiced as a whole group a single time yet, have we?

Ⓑ No, but there's nothing we can do. We'll do it off the cuff.

★ *shōganai (=shikatanai*) = It can't be helped. / There is nothing for it.

2 Ⓐ だめだ、時間切れだ。プレゼンはぶっつけ本番でやるしか
じ かん ぎ　　　　　　　　　　　　　　　　　　　ほんばん
ない。

Dameda, jikan-gire da. Purezen wa buttsuke honban de yaru shika nai.

Ⓑ 大丈夫だよ。きっとうまくいくよ。
だいじょう ぶ

Daijōbu da yo. Kitto umaku iku yo.

Ⓐ It's no good, we're out of time. We'll just have to do the presentation off the cuff.

Ⓑ It's fine. I'm sure it will go well.

★ *purezen* ⇐ presentation

★ *honban* = performance, actual operation

62 目が回る
Me ga mawaru

Makes me feel dizzy

To be so busy that one has no time to rest.

Listen & Speak

1 Ⓐ 忙しくて目が回るよ。
Isogashikute me ga mawaru yo.

Ⓑ 何にも食べてないでしょ。これ、どうぞ。
Nannimo tabetenai desho. Kore, dōzo.

Ⓐ I'm so busy it makes me feel dizzy.
Ⓑ You must not be eating anything. Here, take this.

★ **nannimo ~ nai** = nothing ~ at all

2 Ⓐ この時期はいつも大変。本当に目が回りそうになる。
Kono jiki wa itsumo taihen. Hontō ni me ga mawarisō ni naru.

Ⓑ 私も。
Watashi mo.

Ⓐ This time of year is always tough. Honestly, it almost makes me feel dizzy.
Ⓑ Me too.

★ **jiki** = period, season

顔 face

Useful One-word Expressions in Japanese 17

1. Facial expression 2. Representative 3. Honour, pride
4. Circle of acquaintances, trust

Ex.1) 彼は困った顔をしていた。
He looked upset.

Ex.2) チームの顔
Team representative

Ex.3) 顔をつぶす／顔を立てる
To lose face / to save face

Ex.4) 顔が広い。／顔がきく。
Having many acquaintances. / To have contacts.

Ⓙ Assessing people, describing people as a certain type

Ⓚ To be busy or flustered while acting

Ⓛ To be nervous, to be worried

Ⓜ Differences

Ⓝ Encouraging someone

Ⓞ Dealing with a situation sternly, dealing with a situation gently

Ⓟ Taking criticism, blame, or an attack

Ⓠ Arrogant, proud, or stubborn attitudes

Ⓡ To not match, to become weary, to be fed up

63 息つく暇もない　Not even time to breathe
（いき）（ひま）
Ikitsuku hima mo nai

「息をつく」means "To breathe, to take a short break." To be so
（いき）
busy that you cannot even take a regular breath.

1 **Ⓐ**今、忙しすぎて<u>息つく暇もなくて</u>。もうちょっと待ってく
（いま）（いそが）　　　　（いき）（ひま）　　　　　　　　　　　　　（ま）
れる？

*Ima isogashisugite ikitsuku hima mo nakute. Mō chotto matte
kureru?*

Ⓑわかりました。あまり無理しないでくださいね。
　　　　　　　　　　　　（む）（り）

Wakarimashita. Amari muri shinaide kudasai ne.

Ⓐ I'm so busy I don't even have time to
breathe right now. Could you wait a little
longer?

Ⓑ Understood. Please don't push yourself too
hard.

★ *muri (o) suru* = take it
too far, push oneself

2 **Ⓐ**最近、彼から全然連絡来ないんだけど。
（さいきん）（かれ）　（ぜんぜんれんらくこ）

Saikin, kare kara zenzen renraku konai n da kedo.

Ⓑきっと<u>息つく暇もない</u>ほど忙しいんじゃないかな。今月は
　　　（いき）（ひま）　　　　　（いそが）　　　　　　　　（こんげつ）
すごく忙しくなるって言ってたから。
　　　（いそが）　　　　（い）

*Kitto ikitsuku hima mo nai hodo isogashī n ja nai ka na. Kongetsu
wa sugoku isogashiku naru tte itteta kara.*

Ⓐ He hasn't contacted me at all lately.

Ⓑ He's probably so busy that he doesn't have
time to breathe. He did say that he'd be
extremely busy this month.

★ *sugoku* = awfully, very

64 一夜漬け
いち や づ
Ichiya-zuke

Cram overnight; rush job

A job that was done in a hurry over just one night to make it in time. An expression comparing something to vegetables that have been pickled for only one night.

1 🅐 徹夜して<u>一夜漬け</u>で試験勉強するより、早く寝て朝、勉強
てつや　　　　いちやづ　　　　しけんべんきょう　　　　　　はや　ね　あさ　べんきょう
したほうがいいと思うよ。
おも

Tetsuya shite ichiya-zuke de shiken-benkyō suru yori, hayaku nete asa, benkyō shita hō ga ī to omou yo.

🅑 そう？　じゃ、そうしようかな。

Sō? Ja, sō shiyo ka na.

🅐 Instead of cramming overnight and pulling an all-nighter, I think it would be better to sleep early and study in the morning.

🅑 Really? Then maybe I'll do that.

★ ***sugoku*** = awfully, very

2 🅐 あ、かっこいい！　このポスター、素敵！
すてき

A, kakkoī! Kono posutā, suteki!

🅑 ありがとうございます。<u>一夜漬け</u>で作ったから、あまり自
いちやづ　　　つく　　　　　　　　　　じ
信ないですけど。
しん

Arigatō gozaimasu. Ichiya-zuke de tsukutta kara, amari jishin nai desu kedo.

🅐 Oh, that's so cool! This poster is great!

🅑 Thank you very much. I'm not very confident about it, though, it was a rush job.

★ ***kakkoī*** = cool
★ ***suteki (na)*** = fantastic

65 手に汗握る
（て）（あせ）（にぎ）
Te ni ase nigiru

To have sweaty palms; breathtaking

To be excited and nervous. Used particularly often when expecting some sort of results.

Listen & Speak

1 Ⓐ 昨日の試合、どうだった？
（きのう）（しあい）
Kinō no shiai, dō datta?

Ⓑ 勝ったよ。でも、手に汗握るいい試合だったよ。
（か）　　　　　（て）（あせにぎ）　　　（しあい）
Katta yo. Demo, te ni ase nigiru ī shiai datta yo.

Ⓐ How was yesterday's match?
Ⓑ We won. But it was such a close game I could feel my palms sweating.

★ *katsu* = win

2 Ⓐ すごい試合だね。
（しあい）
Sugoi shiai da ne.

Ⓑ うん、手に汗握るよ。
（て）（あせにぎ）
Un, te ni ase nigiru yo.

Ⓐ What an incredible match.
Ⓑ Yeah, it's thrilling!

★ *sugoi* = amazing, terrible

受ける（ウケる）　**Useful One-word Expressions in Japanese 18**
（う）　　　　　　to receive, get

To be favourably received, to get a good response

Ex.) 冗談を言ったら、受けた。／子供に受けた。／受ける話をしてほしい。
（じょうだん）（い）　　（う）　　（こども）（う）　　　（う）　　（はなし）
When he made a joke, it got a good reaction. / The children liked it.
/ I want you to make a speech that everyone will like.

66 気が気でない

き き

Feel uneasy

Ki ga ki de nai

To feel anxious, worried, and not calm because of something you are concerned about.

J Assessing people, describing people as a certain type

K To be busy or flustered while acting

L To be nervous, to be worried

M Differences

N Encouraging someone

O Dealing with a situation sternly, dealing with a situation gently

P Taking criticism, blame, or an attack

Q Arrogant, proud or stubborn attitudes

R To not match, to become weary, to be fed up

1 **Ⓐ** 結婚式なのに、けんかを始めて……。見ていて気が気じゃ
けっこんしき はじ み き き
なかったよ。

Kekkon-shiki na noni, kenka o hajimete .... Mite ite ki ga ki ja nakatta yo.

Ⓑ ごめん、ごめん、心配かけて。けんかっていうわけじゃな
しんぱい
いんだよ。

Gomen, gomen, sinpai kakete. Kenka tte yū wake ja nai n da yo.

Ⓐ Starting to fight, even though it's your wedding ceremony...? Just watching you made me feel uneasy.

Ⓑ Sorry for making you worry. It's not like we were really fighting.

★ ***shinpai o kakeru*** = cause anxiety to, cause someone to worry

---

2 **Ⓐ** 明日のイベント、雨降ったら、どうします？
あした あめ ふ

Ashita no ibento, ame futtara, dō shimasu?

Ⓑ そんなこと言うなよ。それでなくても客が少ないんじゃな
い きゃく すく
いかって気が気じゃないんだから。
き き

Sonna koto yū na yo. Sore de nakutemo kyaku ga sukunai n ja naika tte ki ga ki ja nai n da kara.

Ⓐ What will you do if it rains during tomorrow's event?

Ⓑ Don't say something like that. I'm already feeling uneasy that not many people will come.

★ ***ibento*** = event

67 居てもたってもいられない

Ite mo tatte mo irarenai　　　Itching to do something

To feel annoyed, anxious, and unsettled because something weighs on your mind.

1 Ⓐ どうしたの？　さっきから立ったり座ったりして。

Dōshita no? Sakki kara tattari suwattari shite.

Ⓑ 面接を受けた会社から今日、電話かかってくる予定なんだ。

Mensetsu o uketa kaisha kara kyō, denwa kakatte kuru yotē na n da.

- - - - - - - - - - - - - - - - - - - -

Ⓐ What's the matter? You've been standing and sitting over and over for a bit now.

Ⓑ I'm supposed to get a call from the company I interviewed at today.

★ **yotē** = schedule

2 Ⓐ ちょっと駅まで迎えに行ってくる。うちで待ってても、<u>居てもたってもいられない</u>から。

Chotto eki made mukae ni itte kuru. Uchi de mattete mo, ite mo tatte mo irarenai kara.

Ⓑ わかった。

Wakatta.

- - - - - - - - - - - - - - - - - - - -

Ⓐ I'm going to the station to meet them there. I'll just be itching to do something if I stay here at home.

Ⓑ All right.

★ **mukae ni iku** = go to pick up, go to meet

J Assessing people, describing people as a certain type

K To be busy or flustered while acting

L To be nervous, to be worried

M Differences

N Encouraging someone

O Dealing with a situation sternly, dealing with a situation gently

P Taking criticism, blame, or an attack

Q Arrogant, proud, or stubborn attitudes

R To become weary, to be fed up

68 食事がのどを通らない
しょく じ　　　　　　　　　とお

Shokuji ga nodo o tōranai　　　Can't eat a bite

To not have any appetite due to heartbreak, worry, fatigue, or so on.

Listen & Speak

1 Ⓐ彼、どんな様子？
かれ　　　　　　よう す

Kare, donna yōsu?

Ⓑ かなり不安そうな感じ。検査結果が出るまで<u>食事ものどを</u>
ふ あん　　　かん　　　けん さ けっ か　　で　　　　しょく じ
<u>通らない</u>みたい。
とお

Kanari fuan sō na kanji. Kensa-kekka ga deru made shokuji mo nodo o tōranai mitai.

Ⓐ How is he doing?

Ⓑ He seems fairly worried. It doesn't seem like he'll be able to eat a bite until the exam results come back.

★ *yōsu* = state, condition, appearance

★ *kensa* = inspection, checkup

2 Ⓐ彼女、失恋で<u>食事がのどを通らない</u>んだって。
かの じょ　　しつ れん　　しょく じ　　　　とお

Kanojo, shitsuren de shokuji ga nodo o tōranai n da tte.

Ⓑ そう言えば、ちょっとやせたね。
い

Sō ieba, chotto yaseta ne.

Ⓐ It seems like she can't eat a bite because of her broken heart.

Ⓑ Now that you mention it, she has lost a little bit of weight.

★ *shitsuren* = lost love

★ *sō ieba* = come to think of it

CD 35

69 月と<ruby>月<rt>つき</rt></ruby>スッポン
<ruby>月<rt>つき</rt></ruby>とスッポン
Tsuki to suppon

Like chalk and cheese; like the moon and a turtle

A comparison between things that look similar at first glance but are actually incomparably different. As a turtle's shell is round, it is sometimes called 「<ruby>丸<rt>まる</rt></ruby>」. The phrase comes from the fact that the moon is also round, and when reflected in water it may look the same as a turtle in the mud. It compares the moon, a beautiful object, and a turtle, an ugly object.

Listen & Speak

1 Ⓐ<ruby>同<rt>おな</rt></ruby>じ<ruby>兄弟<rt>きょうだい</rt></ruby>でも<u>月とスッポン</u>だよ。<ruby>兄<rt>あに</rt></ruby>は<ruby>勉強<rt>べんきょう</rt></ruby>もスポーツもできるけど、<ruby>弟<rt>おとうと</rt></ruby>の<ruby>僕<rt>ぼく</rt></ruby>は<ruby>何<rt>なに</rt></ruby>をやっても<ruby>普通以下<rt>ふつういか</rt></ruby>。

Onaji kyōdai demo tsuki to suppon da yo. Ani wa benkyō mo supōtsu mo dekiru kedo, otōto no boku wa nani o yatte mo futsū ika.

Ⓑそんなことないって。

Sonna koto nai tte.

> Ⓐ We may be brothers, but we're like chalk and cheese. My older brother is good at studying and at sports, but I'm below average no matter what I do.
>
> Ⓑ That's not true.

> ★ **futsū** = normal, ordinary, average
>
> ★ **~ ika** = below ~

2 Ⓐ<ruby>彼<rt>かれ</rt></ruby>と<ruby>同<rt>おな</rt></ruby>じ<ruby>大学<rt>だいがく</rt></ruby>なんだってね。

Kare to onaji daigaku na n da tte ne.

Ⓑええ、まあ。でも、<ruby>彼<rt>かれ</rt></ruby>と<ruby>私<rt>わたくし</rt></ruby>では<u>月とスッポン</u>ですよ。<ruby>彼<rt>かれ</rt></ruby>は<ruby>一流企業<rt>いちりゅうきぎょう</rt></ruby>の<ruby>経営者<rt>けいえいしゃ</rt></ruby>、<ruby>僕<rt>ぼく</rt></ruby>は<ruby>小<rt>ちい</rt></ruby>さい<ruby>会社<rt>かいしゃ</rt></ruby>のサラリーマンですから。

Ē, mā. Demo, kare to watashi dewa tsuki to suppon desu yo. Kare wa ichiryū kigyō no kēēsha, boku wa chīsai kaisha no sararīman desu kara.

> Ⓐ So he went to the same university as you.
>
> Ⓑ Yes, I suppose. But he and I are like chalk and cheese. He's the proprietor of a first-rate corporation, while I'm a salary man at a small company.

> ★ **ichiryū** = first class, topnotch

J Assessing people, describing people as a certain type

K To be busy or flustered while acting

L To be nervous, to be worried

M Differences

N Encouraging someone

O Dealing with a situation strongly, feeling with a situation gently

P Taking criticism, blame, or an attack

Q Arrogant, proud or stubborn attitudes

R To not match, to become weary, to be fed up

70 ピンからキリまで

From worst to best; large range

Pin kara kiri made

From the lowest possible level to the highest possible level. Used in reference not just to goods, but to people, organizations, and various other things. A reference to Tensho karuta cards, based on Portuguese playing cards that came into Japan from the West. ピン is a 1, and キリ is the highest value, a 12.

Listen & Speak

1 Ⓐお土産にお茶を買おうと思うんですが。

O-miyage ni o-cha o kaō to omou n desu ga.

Ⓑあ、そう。でも、お茶も<u>ピンからキリまで</u>あるからね。どれぐらいのものがいいの？

A, sō. Demo, o-cha mo pin kara kiri made aru kara ne. Dore gurai no mono ga ī no?

Ⓐ I'm thinking of getting tea as a souvenir.
Ⓑ Oh, I see. But there's a whole range of teas. About how much do you want to spend?

★ *o-miyage* = souvenir

2 Ⓐ〈パンフレットを見ながら〉

ホテルも<u>ピンからキリまで</u>あるね。

〈*Panfuretto o minagara*〉

Hoteru mo pin kara kiri made aru ne.

Ⓑうん。でも１泊１万円までにしたいな。

Un. Demo ippaku ichi-man-en made ni shitai na.

Ⓐ 〈While looking at a pamphlet〉
There's certainly a large range of hotels.
Ⓑ Yes. But I'd like to keep it to 10,000 yen a night at most.

★ *panfuretto* = brochure
★ *~ haku (paku)* = ~night

71　雲泥の差
うんでい　さ
Undē no sa

A world of difference

To have a clear difference in ability, evaluation, and so on. Comes from the fact that clouds and mud are nothing alike.

Listen & Speak

1 Ⓐ 食べていただくとわかるんですが、ほかのお肉とは<u>雲泥の差</u>がありますよ。
た　　　　　　　　　　　　　　　　　　　にく　　　うんでい　さ

　Tabete itadaku to wakaru n desu ga, hoka no o-niku to wa undē no sa ga arimasu yo.

Ⓑ そうですか。

　Sō desu ka.

Ⓐ You'll understand if you eat it, but there's a world of difference between it and other meat.

Ⓑ Is that so?

★ ***o-niku*** = meat

2 Ⓐ 〈掃除機について〉
　　　そうじき

これとそれはそんなに違うんですか。
　　　　　　　　　　　ちが

　〈*Sojiki ni tsuite*〉
　Kore to sore wa sonna ni chigau n desu ka.

Ⓑ それはもう、<u>雲泥の差</u>です。パワーが全然違いますから。
　　　　　　　うんでい　さ　　　　　　　　　ぜんぜんちが

　Sore wa mō, undē no sa desu. Pāwa ga zenzen chigaimasu kara.

Ⓐ (About a vacuum cleaner) Are these two that different?

Ⓑ Yes, it's a world of difference. The power they have is completely different.

★ ***sōjiki*** = vacuum cleaner

72 足元にも及ばない Doesn't hold a candle to
Ashimoto nimo oyobanai

To be incomparable due to completely different levels of ability or results. Often used about yourself to be modest.

1 Ⓐ青木さんもゴルフやるんですか。

Aoki-san mo gorufu yaru n desu ka?

Ⓑはい。でも、私なんか田中さんの<u>足元にも及ばない</u>ですよ。すごく下手ですから。

Hai. Demo, watashi nanka Tanaka-san no ashimoto nimo oyobanai desu yo. Sugoku heta desu kara.

Ⓐ Do you play golf too, Aoki-san?
Ⓑ Yes, but I don't hold a candle to Tanaka-san. I'm awful.

★ *heta (na)* = be poor/bad at

2 Ⓐうちの子なんか、お宅のお子さんの<u>足元にも及びません</u>よ。とにかく、勉強しませんから。

Uchi no ko nanka, o-taku no o-ko-san no ashimoto nimo oyobimasen yo. Tonikaku, benkyō shimasen kara.

Ⓑいえいえ、そんなことないでしょう。

Ieie, sonna koto nai deshō.

Ⓐ Our child doesn't hold a candle to yours. He simply doesn't study.
Ⓑ No, of course that isn't true.

★ *o-taku* = a polite expression of "you", "your family" or "your home"

CD
37

73

上には上がある
うえ　　うえ
Ue niwa ue ga aru

There's always someone better

An expression that says that even if you think something is the greatest or superior, there is always something greater. Often used to warn someone acting conceited, or to be modest.

1 Ⓐ すごい！　彼ら、全員Ｎ１合格なんだって。
かれ　　ぜんいん　　ごうかく

Sugoi! karera, zen'in Enu-ichi gōkaku na n da tte.

Ⓑ 上には上がいるね。私なんか、Ｎ２でちょっと自慢してたけど。
うえ　　うえ　　　　　わたし　　　　　　　　　　　　　じまん

Ue niwa ue ga iru ne. Watashi nanka Enu-ni de chotto jiman shiteta kedo.

Ⓐ That's amazing! They all passed N1.
Ⓑ I guess there's always someone better. I was boasting a bit over N2, after all.

★ **zen'in** = all the menbers, everybody
★ **jiman suru** = boast, take pride in

2 Ⓐ 今回は優勝できましたけど、上には上がいます。出場しな
こんかい　ゆうしょう　　　　　　　　　うえ　　うえ　　　　　　しゅつじょう
かった選手ですごい人いますから。
せんしゅ　　　　　ひと

Konkai wa yūshō dekimashita kedo, ue niwa ue ga imasu. Shutsujō shinakatta senshu de sugoi hito imasu kara.

Ⓑ でも、優勝は立派だよ。
ゆうしょう　りっぱ

Demo yūshō wa rippa da yo.

Ⓐ I may have won this time, but there's always someone better. There are some incredible people who didn't enter.
Ⓑ But it's splendid that you won.

★ **yūshō suru** = win a championship
★ **shutsujō suru** = participate in

J Assessing people, describing people as a certain type

K To be busy or flustered while acting

L To be nervous, to be worried

M Differences

N Encouraging someone

O Dealing with a situation sternly, dealing with a situation gently

P Taking criticism, blame, or an attack

Q Arrogant, proud or stubborn attitudes

R To not match, to become weary, to be fed up

74 勝ち組・負け組
Kachigumi / Makegumi

Winner / Loser

An expression used to classify people as winners or losers based on their success by social standards such as their academic record, promotions, income, marriage, and so on.

Listen & Speak

1 Ⓐ最近、勝ち組・負け組っていう言葉よく聞くね。
Saikin, kachigumi / makegumi tte yū kotoba yoku kiku ne.

Ⓑなんだかお金がすべてみたいな分け方で好きじゃないな。
Nandaka o-kane ga subete mitai na wakekata de suki ja nai na.

Ⓐ You hear people talking about winners and losers a lot lately.

Ⓑ I don't like it when people seem to divide people as if money is everything.

★ **nandaka ~** = somehow ~, I don't know, why ~

2 Ⓐ僕なんか、給料はよくないし、彼女いないし。完全に負け組だよね。
Boku nanka, kyūryō wa yokunai shi, kanojo inai shi. Kanzen ni makegumi da yo ne.

Ⓑそんなことないよ。
Sonna koto nai yo.

Ⓐ A: I don't have a good salary, and I don't have a girlfriend either. I'm a total loser.

Ⓑ That's not true.

★ **kanzen ni** = completely, entirely

75 肩を持つ
<small>かた　も</small>
Kata o motsu

To side with

To take someone's side, to support someone emotionally.

1 Ⓐ〈姉の不平〉
<small>あね　ふ へい</small>

お父さんはいつもまり子の<u>肩を持つ</u>んだから。
<small>とう　　　　　　　　こ　　かた　も</small>

〈*Ane no fuhē*〉
Otōsan wa itsumo Mariko no kata o motsu n da kara.

Ⓑそんなことないよ。お父さんは公平だよ。
<small>とう　　　　こうへい</small>

Sonna koto nai yo. Otōsan wa kōhē da yo.

Ⓐ (An older sister's complaint) Dad always sides with Mariko.
Ⓑ That's not true. He's fair.

★ ***fuhē*** = discontent
★ ***kōhē (na)*** = fair

2 Ⓐ君はどっちの側？
<small>きみ　　　　　がわ</small>

Kimi wa docchi no gawa?

Ⓑどっちでもないよ。どっちかの<u>肩を持つ</u>のは、いやだな。
<small>かた　も</small>

Docchi de mo nai yo. Docchika no kata o motsu no wa iya da na.

Ⓐ Which side are you on?
Ⓑ I'm not on either side. I don't like taking sides.

★ ***gawa*** = side

76 尻を叩く
しり たた
Shiri o tataku

Kick in the pants

To forcefully urge someone to take action, or to spur them on.

Listen & Speak

1

Ⓐ 締め切りが近いのに全然やってないんだって？
し き ちか ぜんぜん
Shimekiri ga chikai no ni zenzen yatte nai n da tte?

Ⓑ うん……。先生にさっき尻を叩かれたよ。
せんせい しり たた
Un.... Sensē ni sakki shiri o tatakareta yo.

Ⓐ You haven't done any of it even though the due date is coming up?

Ⓑ No... Our teacher just gave me a kick in the pants.

★ *shimekiri* = deadline

2

Ⓐ 彼、のんきだから、早くやるようにって尻を叩いてきました。
かれ はや しり たた
Kare, nonki da kara, hayaku yaru yō ni tte shiri o tataite kimashita.

Ⓑ そう。それは助かった。ありがとう。
たす
Sō. Sore wa tasukatta. Arigatō.

Ⓐ He's easygoing, so I gave him a kick in the pants telling him to do it soon.

Ⓑ Oh. I'm glad you did, thank you.

★ *nonki (na)*= easygoing
★ *tasukaru* = be helped

落ちる to fall
お

Useful One-word Expressions in Japanese 19

1. To disappear from somewhere   2. To fail a test

Ex.1) 汚れが落ちる／色が落ちる／化粧が落ちる
よご お いろ お けしょう お
Dirt comes out / colour fades / make-up comes off

Ex.2) 試験に落ちる／面接に落ちる
し けん お めんせつ お
To fail a test / to fail an interview

77 水に流す
みず なが
Mizu ni nagasu

Water under the bridge;
to forgive and forget

To act like past troubles never happened.
For more information, refer to the column.

Listen & Speak

1 Ⓐ 本当にいろいろご迷惑をおかけして申し訳ありません。反省してます。

Hontō ni iroiro go-mēwaku o o-kake shite mōshiwake arimasen. Hansē shite imasu.

Ⓑ まあ、今回だけは<u>水に流し</u>ましょう。

Mā, konkai dake wa mizu ni nagashimashō.

Ⓐ I'm truly sorry for causing you so much trouble. I'm reflecting on what I've done.

Ⓑ Well, we can call it water under the bridge this time.

★ *mēwaku o kakeru* = cause someone trouble

★ *hansē suru* = reflect on

2 Ⓐ いろいろあったけど、<u>水に流して</u>、また最初からやり直しましょう。

Iroiro atta kedo, mizu ni nagashite, mata saisho kara yarinaoshi mashō.

Ⓑ ありがとうございます。

Arigatō gozaimasu

Ⓐ I know a lot has happened, but let's call it water under the bridge and start over from the beginning.

Ⓑ Thank you.

★ *yarinaosu* = do something (over) again

78 なかったことにする

Nakatta koto ni suru

Pretend it never happened;
let bygones be bygones

To take back something mid-way that has begun to happen or that
has been decided upon through discussions. Often used when
calling something off in negotiations.

1 Ⓐ すみません、これまでの話、<u>なかったことにさせて</u>くださ
い。社の方針が変わったんです。

*Sumimasen, kore made no hanashi, nakatta koto ni sasete
kudasai. Sha no hōshin ga kawatta n desu.*

Ⓑ えっ、そんな……。

Ett, sonna....

> Ⓐ I'm sorry, let's please pretend our
> discussions until now never happened.
> Our company's policies have changed.
> Ⓑ What? You can't say that....

★ **sha (=kaisha)** = my company
★ **hōshin** = policy, line

2 Ⓐ 例の食事会ですが、いつがいいですか。

Rē no shokuji-kai desu ga, itsu ga ī desu ka.

Ⓑ ああ、あの話、悪いけど、<u>なかったことにして</u>くれません
か。彼女が行かないって言い出して。

*Ā, ano hanashi, warui kedo, nakatta koto ni shite kuremasen ka?
Kanojo ga ikanai tte ī dashite.*

> Ⓐ When should we have that meal we were
> talking about?
> Ⓑ Oh, about that. Sorry, but could you
> pretend that never happened? My
> girlfriend started saying she won't go.

★ **rē no** = that
★ **rē no ~ desu ga** = regarding
  that ~

79 大目に見る
おおめ み
Ōme ni miru

To overlook

To understand a situation or circumstances, and to act with leniency about something that would normally be blamed or criticized.

 Listen & Speak

1 ⓐ本当に申し訳ありませんでした。
ほんとう もう わけ
Hontō ni mōshiwake arimasendeshita.

ⓑまあ、まだ慣れてないし、今回は大目に見ましょう。
な こんかい おおめ み
Mā, mada naretenai shi, konkai wa ōme ni mimashō.

ⓐ I'm truly sorry.
ⓑ Well, you haven't gotten the hang of it yet. I'll overlook it this time.

★ **nareru** = get used to

2 すみません、もう二度と同じことはしませんので、今度だけ大
に ど おな こんど おお
目に見てください。
め み
Sumimasen, mō nidoto onaji koto wa shimasen node, kondo dake ōme ni mite kudasai.

I'm sorry, I won't ever do it again. Please overlook it this one time.

★ **(mō) nido to ~ nai** = never ~ again

目 eye
め

Useful One-word Expressions in Japanese 20

1. Eyesight 2. Attention 3. Impression, appearance 4. Seeing, meeting 5. Experience
6. (Used with a verb or adjective) a condition like that 7. To be in order

Ex.1) 私は目が悪いです。
わたし め わる
My eyesight is bad.

Ex.2) 周りの目
まわ め
Attention from people around one

Ex.3) 見た目がいい
み め
Something looks good.

Ex.4) 先生にお目にかかりました。
せんせい め
I met the teacher.

Ex.5) ひどい目にあった。
め
I had a terrible experience.

Ex.6) 少なめにしてください。
すく
Please make it a small amount.

Ex.7) 二つ目の駅で降りる
ふた め えき お
To get off at the second station

80 長い目で見る
_{なが} _め _み
Nagai me de miru

Look at the long term

To judge something not only based on the current situation but over a longer period of time into the future.

1

Ⓐあいつは使えないよ。何もわかっていない。
_{つか} _{なに}

Aitsu wa tsukaenai yo. Nani mo wakatte inai.

Ⓑ確かに、若いからまだまだですが、どうか長い目で見てやっ
_{たし} _{わか} _{なが} _め _み
てください。

Tashika ni, wakai kara madamada desu ga, dōka nagai me de mite yatte kudasai.

Ⓐ He's useless. He doesn't understand a thing.

Ⓑ Yes, he may have a long way to go because he's young, but please, look at him in the long term.

★ *aitsu* = a casual, often rough way of referring to another person

★ *tashika ni* = to be sure, indeed, it is true that

2

Ⓐこれ、高いけど、丈夫だから長い目で見たら、安いかもし
_{たか} _{じょう ぶ} _{なが} _め _み _{やす}
れないよ。

Kore, takai kedo, jōbu da kara nagai me de mitara, yasui kamo shirenai yo.

Ⓑ確かにそうだね。
_{たし}

Tashikani sō da ne.

Ⓐ This may be expensive, but it's durable. So it may be cheap when you look at the long term.

Ⓑ You know, you're right.

★ *jōbu (na)* = strong, robust, durable

J Assessing people, describing people as a certain type

K To be busy or flustered while acting

L To be nervous, to be worried

M Differences

N Encouraging someone

O Dealing with a situation sternly, dealing with a situation gently

P Talking criticism, blame, or an attack

Q Arrogant, proud or stubborn attitudes

R To not match, to become weary, to be fed up

O | Dealing with a situation sternly, dealing with a situation gently

 CD 41

81 心を鬼にして
こころ　おに
Kokoro o oni ni shite

Harden one's heart

To act in a stern way for someone's sake despite wanting to deal with them kindly. Often used in an educational setting.

Listen & Speak

1 **Ⓐ** 孫はかわいいけど、甘やかすのはよくないから、心を鬼にして叱ることもあります。
まご　　　　　　　あま　　　　　　　　　　　　こころ　おに　　　　　しか

Mago wa kawaī kedo, amayakasu no wa yokunai kara, kokoro o oni ni shite sikaru koto mo arimasu.

Ⓑ そうですか。

Sō desu ka.

Ⓐ My grandchildren are cute, but it's not good to spoil them, so sometimes I harden my heart and scold them.

Ⓑ Is that so.

★ **amayakasu** = pamper, spoil

2 **Ⓐ** 彼にまたお金貸したの？
かれ　　　　かね　か

Kare ni mata o-kane kashita no?

Ⓑ いや。今回は心を鬼にして断ったよ。
こんかい　こころ　おに　　　ことわ

Iya. Konkai wa kokoro o oni ni shite kotowatta yo.

Ⓐ You lent him money again?

Ⓑ No. I hardened my heart this time and said no.

★ **kotowaru** = turn down, refuse

送る to send
おく

Useful One-word Expressions in Japanese 21

I. To accompany someone to a certain place　2. To dispatch, send

Ex.1) 駅まで妹を送る／車で友達を送る
えき　いもうと　おく　　くるま　ともだち　おく
To take one's sister to the station / To drive a friend somewhere

Ex.2) スタッフを送る／エンジニアを送る
おく　　　　　　　　　　おく
Dispatch staff / send an engineer

82

百歩譲って
ひゃっ ぽ ゆず
Hyappo yuzutte

Unwillingly give in

To broadly accept someone's point. A metaphor saying that one is making someone else move forward a hundred steps before broadly accepting their point.

1 ⓐ そういう約束はしてないです。
やくそく
Sō yū yakusoku wa shitenai desu.

ⓑ そうですか。まあ、<u>百歩譲って</u>約束はしてないとしても、
ひゃっ ぽ ゆず やくそく
この結果には責任あるんじゃないですか。
けっか せきにん
Sō desu ka. Mā hyappo yuzutte yakusoku wa shite nai to shite mo, kono kekka niwa sekinin aru n ja nai desu ka?

ⓐ I haven't made that kind of promise.

ⓑ Is that so. Well, even if I do unwillingly state that you didn't make a promise, aren't you still responsible for these results?

★ *sekinin* = responsibility

2 相手が一方的に悪いと思うけど、<u>百歩譲って</u>、こちらも悪かっ
あいて いっぽうてき わる おも ひゃっ ぽ ゆず わる
たということにしよう。

Aite ga ippōteki ni warui to omou kedo, hyappo yuzutte, kochira mo warukatta to yū koto ni shiyō.

While I do think they were entirely in the wrong, I will unwillingly accept that I'm somewhat to blame.

★ *ippōteki ni* = one-sidedly, unilaterally

83 叩かれる

たた
Tatakareru

Abused

When many negative opinions appear regarding one's words or actions, making one the target of criticism. 「叩く」 indicates the beating of a body with one's hands or an object, and this term uses the idea in a psychological sense.

Listen & Speak

1 Ⓐ あの議員、テレビとかネットとかでずいぶん<u>叩かれてる</u>ね。
ぎ いん　　　　　　　　　　　　　　　　　　たた
Ano gīn, terebi toka netto toka de zuibun tatakareteru ne.

Ⓑ 当然だよ、あんな差別発言したんだもの。
とうぜん　　　　　さ べつはつげん
Tōzen da yo, anna sabetsu-hatsugen shita n da mono.

Ⓐ That diet member is getting quite abused on TV and the Internet, isn't he?

Ⓑ Of course he is, after he made that discriminatory remark.

★ **giin** = member of an assembly

★ **sabetsu-hatsugen** = discriminatory remark

2 Ⓐ どうしたの？　ため息なんかついて。
いき
Dō shita no? Tameiki nanka tsuite.

Ⓑ うん……。会議で反対意見を言ったら、みんなから<u>叩かれ</u>ちゃって。
かい ぎ　　はんたい い けん　 い　　　　　　　　　　　　たた
Un .... Kaigi de hantai-iken o ittara, minna kara tatakarechatte.

Ⓐ What's the matter? Why are you sighing?

Ⓑ Well... I raised an objection at the meeting, and everyone started giving me abuse about it.

★ **tameiki o tsuku** = sigh, heave a sigh

J Assessing people, describing people as a certain type

K To be busy or flustered while acting

L To be nervous, to be worried

M Differences

N Encouraging someone

O Dealing with a situation sternly, dealing with a situation gently

P Taking criticism, blame, or an attack

Q Arrogant, proud, or stubborn attitudes

R To not match, to become weary, to be fed up

84 風当たりが強い
かぜ あ　　　　つよ
Kaze-atari ga tsuyoi

Strongly criticized ; looked down upon

To be unappreciated by society and the target of much criticism. The term takes the idea of being physically hit by strong winds and applies it in a psychological manner.

Listen & Speak

1 Ⓐ以前は男の選手が髪を染めると<u>風当たりが強かった</u>です
いぜん　おとこ　せんしゅ　かみ　そ　　　　　かぜ あ　　　　つよ
が、最近ではそうでもないですね。
さいきん

Izen wa otoko no senshu ga kami o someru to kaze-atari ga tsuyokatta desu ga, saikin dewa sō demo nai desu ne.

Ⓑそうですね。変わりましたね。
か

Sō desu ne. Kawarimashita ne.

Ⓐ Male players who dyed their hair used to be strongly criticized, but that's not true any longer, is it?

Ⓑ You're right, things have changed.

★ *izen wa* = before, previously
★ *kami o someru* = dye one's hair

2 Ⓐ彼、この前、かなり言いたいこと言ってたけど、周りの
かれ　　　まえ　　　　　　い　　　　　い　　　　　　まわ
反応はどう？
はんのう

Kare, kono mae, kanari ītai koto itteta kedo, mawari no hannō wa dō?

Ⓑ大変そうです。すごく<u>風当たりが強くて</u>、本人もまいって
たいへん　　　　　　　　かぜ あ　　　　つよ　　　ほんにん
ますよ。

Taihen sō desu. Sugoku kaze-atari ga tsuyokute, honnin mo maitte masu yo.

Ⓐ It seems hard for him. He was strongly criticized for saying that, and he doesn't know what to do, himself.

Ⓑ It seems hard for him. He was really looked down upon for saying that, and he doesn't know what to do, himself.

★ *hannō* = reaction
★ *mairu* = crack up, be exhausted

103

85 後ろ指を指される
うし ゆび さ
Ushiro-yubi o sasareru

Talked about behind one's back

To have negative things said about you in the shadows without your knowledge. Comes from the image of people speaking ill of you while pointing at you from behind.

Listen & Speak

1 ❶ 人から後ろ指を指されるようなことはしてないよ。
ひと　　　うし ゆび さ
Hito kara ushiro-yubi o sasareru yō na koto wa shitenai yo.

❷ それはわかってるよ。でも、悪く言う人もいるんだよ。
わる い ひと
Sore wa wakatteru yo. Demo, waruku yū hito mo iru n da yo.

> ❶ I haven't done anything that would cause people to talk about me behind my back.
>
> ❷ I know that. But there are still people who badmouth others.

★ *waruku iu(yū)* = speak ill of

2 ❶ ちょっとぐらい、いいんじゃない？　もらっておけば？
Chotto gurai, ī n ja nai? Moratte okeba?

❷ そんなお金いらないよ。後ろ指、指されるのはごめんだよ。
かね　　　　　　　うし ゆび さ
Sonna o-kane iranai yo. Ushiro-yubi, sasareru no wa gomen da yo.

> ❶ Why don't you take a little bit? What's the matter?
>
> ❷ I don't need that kind of money. I don't want people talking about me behind my back.

★ *(~ wa) iranai* = I don't need ~

厳しい strict
きび

Useful One-word Expressions in Japanese

It's hard to do that, It's difficult

Ex.) 水曜は厳しいなあ。木曜じゃ、だめ？
すいよう きび もくよう
／5000円じゃ厳しいから、3000円にして。
えん きび えん
Wednesday's difficult. How about Thursday? /I can't afford ¥5,000. Make it ¥3.000.

86 出る杭は打たれる
で くい う

The nail that sticks up gets hammered down

Deru kui wa utareru

The idea that standing out makes one the target of hatred and jealousy. The term indicates that nails that stick up are hammered so that they no longer stand out.

1 Ⓐ彼、なんか嫌われてるね。
かれ きら

Kare, nanka kirawareteru ne.

Ⓑ出る杭は打たれるからね。新人なのに、自分の意見を主張
で くい う しんじん じ ぶん い けん しゅちょう
しすぎなんだよ。

Deru kui wa utareru kara ne. Shinjin na noni, jibun no iken o shuchō shisugi nan da yo.

Ⓐ It seems like people hate him.

Ⓑ Well, the nail that sticks up gets hammered down. He's new here, but he still insists on his own opinions too much.

★ **shinjin** = new face, rookie
★ **shuchō suru** = assert, claim

---

2 Ⓐ日本だと出る杭は打たれるけど、外国だと逆に評価される
に ほん で くい う がいこく ぎゃく ひょう か
こと、多いんじゃない？
おお

Nihon da to deru kui wa utareru kedo, gaikoku da to gyaku ni hyōka sareru koto, ōi n ja nai?

Ⓑそうだね。

Sō da ne.

Ⓐ The nail that sticks up gets hammered down in Japan, but don't people overseas often get praised for just that?

Ⓑ You're right.

★ **gyaku ni** = on the contrary
★ **hyōka suru** = valuate

---

87 白い目で見る
しろ め み
Shiroi me de miru

Give a cold look

To look at someone with cold or malicious eyes. 「白い目」 comes
from the Chinese term 「白眼」.
はくがん

1 Ⓐ やめなよ、そんな格好。人から白い目で見られるよ。
かっこう ひと しろ め み

Yamena yo, sonna kakkō. Hito kara shiroi me de mirareru yo.

Ⓑ 別にいいよ。人の目なんて気にしないから。
べつ ひと め き

Betsu ni ī yo. Hito no me nante ki ni shinai kara.

Ⓐ Stop dressing like that. People are
going to give you a cold look.

Ⓑ It's fine, it's not like I care about what
people think.

★ *~na kakkō o suru* = be
dressed ~

2 Ⓐ そんな白い目で見ないでよ。ちょっと冗談言っただけなん
しろ め み じょうだん い
だから。

*Sonna shiroi me de minaide yo. Chotto jōdan itta dake na n da
kara.*

Ⓑ あ、そう。

A, sō.

Ⓐ Don't give me such a cold look. I was
just making a little joke.

Ⓑ Oh, were you?

★ *jōdan o iu* = tell a joke

88 仲間はずれ
なかま

Nakama-hazure

Ostracized; left out

When one is put at a distance by others within a group they belong to or when they are not allowed into a circle of friends.

Listen & Speak

1 Ⓐ 彼だけ<u>仲間はずれ</u>にしたら、かわいそうだよ。
かれ なかま

Kare dake nakama-hazure ni shitara, kawaisō da yo.

Ⓑ あ、忘れてた。声かけとくよ。
わす こえ

A, wasureteta. Koe kaketoku yo.

> Ⓐ A: I'd feel bad if we ostracized just him.
> Ⓑ B: Oh, I forgot. I'll talk to him.

> ★ **koe o kakeru** =call out to, talk to

2 Ⓐ なんか、私だけ<u>仲間はずれ</u>みたい。
わたし なかま

Nanka, watashi dake nakama-hazure mitai.

Ⓑ そうじゃないよ。すごく忙しそうだし、興味ないかなって
いそが きょうみ
思っただけ。
おも

Sō ja nai yo. Sugoku isogashisō da shi, kyōmi nai kana tte omotta dake.

> Ⓐ A: It feels like I'm being left out.
> Ⓑ B: That's not true. You seem really busy, and we just thought you wouldn't be interested.

> ★ **~ ni kyōmi ga nai** = have no interst in ~

Ⓙ Assessing people, describing people as a certain type

Ⓚ To be busy or flustered while acting

Ⓛ To be nervous, to be worried

Ⓜ Differences

Ⓝ Encouraging someone

Ⓞ Dealing with a situation sternly, dealing with a situation gently

Ⓟ Taking criticism, blame, or an attack

Ⓠ Arrogant, proud, or stubborn attitudes

Ⓡ To not match, to become weary, to be fed up

89 村八分
むらはちぶ
Mura hachi-bu

Outcast

To be ignored by other members of a specific group one belongs to and to not be treated as an equal.

1 Ⓐ勝ってよかったね。
か
Katte yokatta ne.

Ⓑうん。自分が大きなミスをしたからね。このまま負けたら、
じ ぶん おお ま
みんなに村八分になってたかも。
むらはちぶ
Un. Jibun ga ōkina misu o shita kara ne. kono mama maketara, minna ni mura hachi-bu ni natteta kamo.

Ⓐ It's a good thing you won.
Ⓑ Yeah. Because I made a big mietake, if we went on to lose, I might have become an outcast.

★ ***misu o suru*** = make a mistake

2 Ⓐ寮に住むんだったら、誰とでも仲良くしたほうがいいよ。
りょう す だれ なか よ
Ryō ni sumu n dattara, dare to demo nakayoku shita hō ga ī yo.

Ⓑわかってるって。村八分にはなりたくないからね。
むらはちぶ
Wakatteru tte. Mura hachi-bu niwa naritakunai kara ne.

Ⓐ If you're going to live in a dorm, you should get along with everyone.
Ⓑ Yeah, I know. I don't want to become an outcast, after all.

★ ***nakayoku suru*** = get along with, make friends with

90 根も葉もない
ね　　は

Ne mo ha mo nai

Baseless

A story or rumor that has no grounding or reason. When a plant grows, its roots act as its base, and it then grows leaves. This expression describes an absurd situation by comparing it to a plant which has neither roots nor leaves but is still growing, even though it should not be. The expression is often followed with 「話」 or 「噂」.
はなし　　うわさ

1 Ⓐ 彼女、もうすぐ離婚するんだってね。
かのじょ　　　　　　りこん

Kanojo, mōsugu rikon suru n da tte ne.

Ⓑ えー、誰がそんなこと言ったの？　そんな根も葉もない
だれ　　　　　　　　い　　　　　　　　　　ね　　は
話、信じないほうがいいよ。
はなし　しん

Ē, dare ga sonna koto itta no? Sonna ne mo ha mo nai hanashi, shinjinai hō ga ī yo.

Ⓐ I heard she's going to get divorced soon.
Ⓑ What? Who told you that? You shouldn't believe that kind of baseless talk.

★ *rikon suru* = divorce

2 Ⓐ あの居酒屋、残った料理をもう一回出してるって、根も葉
いざかや　　のこ　　りょうり　　　　いっかいだ　　　　　　ね　　は
もないうわさ立てられて、客が減ってるみたい。
た　　　　きゃく　へ

Ano izakaya, nokotta ryōri o mō ikkai dashiteru tte, ne mo ha mo nai uwasa taterarete, kyaku ga hetteru mitai.

Ⓑ そうなんだ。かわいそうに。

Sō nanda. Kawaisō ni.

Ⓐ It sounds like that izakaya is losing customers because of a baseless rumor that they reuse leftover food.
Ⓑ Really? Those poor people.

★ *izakaya* = pub, tavern

109

91 大きな顔をする
おお　　かお

Act like a big shot

Ōkina kao o suru

To have a self-important and cocky attitude. To have a cocky attitude and act like one is important despite not having any ability.

1 Ⓐいい大学を出たからって、大きな顔をしないでほしいね。
だいがく　で　　　　　　　　　おお　　かお

Ī daigaku o deta kara tte, ōkina kao o shinai de hoshī ne.

Ⓑ彼、自分は優秀だと思ってるんだよ。
かれ　じぶん　ゆうしゅう　　　おも

Kare, jibun wa yūshū da to omotteru n da yo.

Ⓐ I wish he wouldn't act like a big shot just because he graduated from a good school.

Ⓑ He thinks that he's talented.

★ *yūshū (na)* = excellent, distinguished

2 Ⓐ彼の態度、ちょっと気になるね。
かれ　たいど　　　　　　　き

Kare no taido, chotto ki ni naru ne.

Ⓑやっぱりそう思う？　新人のくせに、大きな顔しすぎだよね。
おも　　　　しんじん　　　　　おお　　かお

Yappari sō omou? Shinjin no kuse ni, ōkina kao shisugi da yo ne.

Ⓐ His attitude bothers me a little bit.

Ⓑ You too? I think he acts too much like a big shot despite being new, don't you?

★ *taido* = attitude

重い heavy
おも

Useful One-word Expressions in Japanese **23**

1. Serious, not easy　2. Depressed　3. Slow-moving

Ex.1) 重い病気／罪が重い。
おも　びょうき　つみ　おも
Serious illness / serious crime

Ex.2) 気が重い。／重い気持ち
き　おも　　　おも　きも
Depressed. / feeling down

Ex.3) 体が重い。／足が重い。
からだ　おも　　あし　おも
Lethargic. / tired legs

110

92 大きな口をきく
おお　　くち

Ōkina kuchi o kiku

Have a big mouth

To speak out of line without considering one's own position or
ability. Verbs often used after「大きな口」include「きく」and「叩く」.
おお　くち　　　　　　　　　　　たた

Listen & Speak

1 Ⓐ何も知らないやつが<u>大きな口をきく</u>な！
なに　し　　　　　　　　　おお　　くち

Nani mo shiranai yatsu ga ōkina kuchi o kiku na!

Ⓑすみません、余計なことを言いました。
よけい　　　　　　い

Sumimasen, yokēna koto o īmashita.

Ⓐ You shouldn't have such a big
mouth when you don't know
anything!

Ⓑ I'm sorry, I shouldn't have said
that.

★ **yatsu** = a rough way of
speaking referring to someone
with a feeling of despise

★ **yokē (na)** = unnecessary, too
much

---

2 Ⓐ彼は全然だめ。僕だったら、もっとうまくやるのに。
かれ　ぜんぜん　　ぼく

Kare wa zenzen dame. Boku dattara, motto umaku yaru noni.

Ⓑよくそんな<u>大きな口がきける</u>ね。
おお　　くち

Yoku sonna ōkina kuchi ga kikeru ne.

Ⓐ He's no good at all. I would have been
able to do it better.

Ⓑ I can't believe that big mouth of yours.

★ **umaku yaru** = get along
well, do it well

軽い light
かる

Useful One-word Expressions in Japanese 24

1. Not serious　2. Not serious, casual

Ex.1)　軽いけが／軽い病気
かる　　　　かる　びょうき
Slight injury, minor illness

Ex.2)　軽い気持ちで／軽い食事
かる　きも　　　　かる　しょくじ
Light-heartedly／ light meal

J Assessing people, describing people as a certain type

K To be busy or flustered while acting

L To be nervous, to be worried

M Differences

N Encouraging someone

O Dealing with a situation sternly, dealing with a situation gently

P Taking criticism, blame, or an attack

Q Arrogant, proud, or stubborn attitudes

R To not match, to become weary, to be fed up

93 ふんぞりかえる
Funzorikaeru

To have an arrogant and cocky attitude. Comes from the image of someone acting important as they spread out their legs and lean back.

Lean back

Listen & Speak

1 Ⓐ田中さん、部長になったとたんにふんぞりかえって、言い方がすごく偉そうになった。

Tanaka-san, buchō ni natta totan ni funzorikaette, īkata ga sugoku erasō ni natta.

Ⓑ僕もそう思う。

Boku mo sō omou.

Ⓐ The moment Tanaka-san became department chief, he started leaning back and talking like he's so important.

Ⓑ I agree.

★ *erai* = great, admirable

2 Ⓐ電車の中でふんぞり返って座る人、いやだね。

Demsha no naka de funzorikaette suwaru hito, iyada ne.

Ⓑ足、広げてね。迷惑だよね。

Ashi, hirogete ne. Mēwaku da yo ne.

Ⓐ Don't you hate it when people are leaning back in the train?

Ⓑ Yes, with their legs wide open. It's such a nuisance.

★ *hirogeru* = spread, extend

94 鼻で笑う
はな　わら
Hana de warau

Laugh sarcastically

To look down on someone and make a fool of them. From the action of belittling someone by laughing as you breathe out from your nose.

Listen & Speak

1 Ⓐ 昨日話したこと、部長に提案した？
きのう はな　　　　　ぶちょう　ていあん
Kinō hanashita koto, buchō ni tēan shita?

Ⓑ したけど、全然だめ。鼻で笑われただけ。
ぜんぜん　　　　はな　わら
Shitakedo, zenzen dame. Hana de warawareta dake.

Ⓐ Did you propose what we talked about yesterday to the department chief?

Ⓑ I did, but it was no good at all. He just laughed sarcastically.

★ **tēan suru** = suggest, propose

2 Ⓐ なに、鼻で笑ってるの？ 失礼だなあ。
はな　わら　　　　　しつれい
Nani, hana de waratteru no? Shitsurē da nā.

Ⓑ ごめん、ごめん。スーツ着るの、初めて見たから。
き　　　　　はじ　み
Gomen, gomen. Sūtsu kiru no, hajimete mita kara.

Ⓐ Why are you laughing sarcastically at me? That's so rude.

Ⓑ Sorry, sorry. It's just the first time I've seen you wearing a suit.

★ **shitsurē (na)** = rude, discourteous

Ⓙ Assessing people, describing people as a certain type

Ⓚ To be busy or flustered while acting

Ⓛ To be nervous, to be worried

Ⓜ Differences

Ⓝ Encouraging someone

Ⓞ Dealing with a situation sternly, dealing with a situation gently

Ⓟ Taking criticism, blame, or an attack

Ⓠ Arrogant, proud, or stubborn attitudes

Ⓡ To not match, to become weary, to be fed up

95 あぐらをかく

Sit on one's laurels

Agura o kaku

To take a carefree attitude without expending any effort, relying on one's position or authority. 「あぐら」 is a position of sitting on the floor with both knees spread and both legs crossed, and the term comes from the comfort of the position. 「かく」 means "to do."

1 **Ⓐ** ついにみどり銀行がふじ銀行を抜いたね。

Tsuini Midori-ginkō ga Fuji-ginkō o nuita ne.

Ⓑ ふじ銀行はずっと1位だったから、その地位に<u>あぐらをかいてた</u>かもね。

Fuji-ginkō wa zutto ichi-i datta kara, sono chii ni agura o kaiteta kamo ne.

Ⓐ Midori Bank finally overtook Fuji Bank, didn't they?

Ⓑ Fuji Bank has always been #1, so they must have been sitting on their laurels.

★ *nuku* = overtake
★ *chii* = status, position

---

2 うちのホテルは駅の近くだからいつも部屋が埋まるけど、そのことに<u>あぐらをかいて</u>いてはダメだね。

Uci no hoteru wa eki no chikaku da kara itsumo heya ga umaru kedo, sono koto ni agura o kaite wa dame da ne.

Our hotel always has its rooms full because it's close to the station, but we can't allow ourselves to sit on our laurels because of that.

★ *umaru* = be occupied

---

96 あごで使う
つか

Boss around

Ago de tsukau

To take a haughty attitude and use others as one sees fit. Comes from the action of giving orders to people using only one's chin instead of words.

Listen & Speak

1 Ⓐ 店長、ほんとに腹が立つ。
てんちょう　　　　はら　た
Tenchō, honto ni hara ga tatsu.

Ⓑ 人をあごで使うからね。
ひと　　　　　つか
Hito o ago de tsukau kara ne.

Ⓐ The manager really annoys me.
Ⓑ It's because he bosses people around.

★ ***hara ga tatsu*** = get angry

2 Ⓐ 〈会社の新人に〉　先輩たちはどうですか。
かいしゃ しんじん　　　 せんぱい
〈*Kaisha no shinjin ni*〉 *Senpai-tachi wa dō desu ka?*

Ⓑ いろいろ教えてもらってます。あごで使われてますけどね。
おし　　　　　　　　　　　　　　　つか
Iroiro oshiete moratte masu. Ago de tsukawaretemasu kedo ne.

Ⓐ (To a new hire) How are your seniors?
Ⓑ They're teaching me a lot. They are bossing me around, though.

★ ***senpai*** = one's senior

こわす to break　Useful One-word Expressions in Japanese **25**

1. To cause damage to the function (of something) unintentionally

2. To undo something, to bring something back to square one

Ex.1) おなかをこわす／スマホをこわしちゃった。
To have stomach problems/ I broke my Smartphone.

Ex.2) 計画をこわす
けいかく
To ruin a plan

Ⓙ Assessing people, describing people as a certain type

Ⓚ To be busy or flustered while acting

Ⓛ To be nervous, to be worried

Ⓜ Differences

Ⓝ Encouraging someone

Ⓞ Dealing with a situation, dealing with a situation gently

Ⓟ Taking criticism, blame, or an attack

Ⓠ Arrogant, proud, or stubborn attitudes

Ⓡ To not match, to become weary, to be fed up

CD 49

97 格好をつける
Kakkō o tsukeru

Put on airs

To try hard to make oneself look good to others.

Listen & Speak

1 Ⓐ そんなに無理して、格好つけなくていいよ。

Sonna ni muri shite, kakkō tsukenakute ī yo.

Ⓑ 格好なんてつけてないですよ。

Kakkō nante tsuketenai desu yo.

Ⓐ YYou don't need to force yourself and put on airs like that.

Ⓑ I'm not putting on airs.

★ **muri (o) suru** = push oneself

2 Ⓐ あとはぼく一人でやるから、ほかの人はもう帰っていいよ。

Ato wa boku hitori de yaru kara, hoka no hito wa mō kaette ī yo.

Ⓑ どうしたの？　そんなに格好つけちゃって。

Dōshita no? Sonna ni kakkō tsukechatte.

Ⓐ I'll do the rest, so everyone else can leave.

Ⓑ What's the matter? Why are you putting on airs like that?

★ **hoka no hito** = everyone (except me)

うるさい noisy　　　Useful One-word Expressions in Japanese 26

1. It's annoying that there are so many orders. (negative sense)

2. "Particular about …" in the sense of "being careful about.…" (positive sense)

Ex.1) 親がうるさいから、あきらめる。／あの客はいろいろうるさい。
My parents are strict, so I give up. / That customer is fussy about lots of things.

Ex.2) 味にうるさい
Particular about taste

98 聞く耳をもたない Turn a deaf ear
き みみ

Kiku mimi o motanai

To not listen to what others have to say. To not consider the intentions or hopes of others at all.

J Assessing people, describing people, as a certain type

K To be busy or flustered while acting

L To be nervous, to be worried

M Differences

N Encouraging someone

O Dealing with a situation sternly, dealing with a situation gently

P Taking criticism, blame, or an attack

Q Arrogant, proud, or stubborn attitudes

R To not match, to become weary, to be fed up

1 Ⓐ あ〜あ、怒らせちゃったね。
おこ

Āa, okorasechatta ne.

Ⓑ うん……。あの人、ああなると、<u>聞く耳持たなく</u>なるんだ
ひと き みみも
よね。

Un.... Ano hito, ā naru to, kiku mimi motanaku naru n da yo ne.

Ⓐ Ah, it looks like he got mad.
Ⓑ Yeah… Once he's like that, he turns a deaf ear to everything.

★ ***ā naru to*** = that coming

2 Ⓐ 何度も上司を説得しようとしてるんですが、<u>全然聞く耳</u>
なんど じょうし せっとく ぜんぜん き みみ
<u>持って</u>くれないんです。
も

Nando mo jōshi o settoku shiyō to shiteru n desu ga, zenzen kiku mimi motte kurenai n desu.

Ⓑ そうですか。

Sō desu ka.

Ⓐ I tried to convince my boss again and again, but he turned a deaf ear to it all.
Ⓑ Is that so?

★ ***jōshi*** = one's boss

99 足元をみる

<ruby>足元<rt>あしもと</rt></ruby>をみる

Ashimoto o miru

Take advantage of

To find someone's weakness and use it against them.

1

Ⓐ いくら<ruby>頼<rt>たの</rt></ruby>んでも、<ruby>値引<rt>ねび</rt></ruby>きしてくれないんです。

Ikura tanonde mo, nebiki shite kurenai n desu.

Ⓑ むこうはこっちがどうしても<ruby>必要<rt>ひつよう</rt></ruby>だって、わかってるんだよ。だから、<u>足元を見る</u>。

Mukō wa kocchi ga dōshitemo hitsuyōda tte, wakatteru n da yo. Dakara, ashimoto o miru.

Ⓐ He won't give me a discount no matter how much I ask.

Ⓑ It's because they know we need to have it. That's why they're taking advantage of us.

★ **nebiki suru** = discount

2

Ⓐ <ruby>高<rt>たか</rt></ruby>い！ それ、<ruby>普通<rt>ふつう</rt></ruby>の２<ruby>倍<rt>ばい</rt></ruby>だよ。

Takai! Sore, futsū no ni-bai da yo.

Ⓑ うん……。<ruby>荷物<rt>にもつ</rt></ruby>をたくさん<ruby>持<rt>も</rt></ruby>ってるときに、<ruby>急<rt>きゅう</rt></ruby>に<ruby>雨<rt>あめ</rt></ruby>が<ruby>降<rt>ふ</rt></ruby>ってきて……。<u>足元を見られた</u>んだね。

Un.... Nimotsu o takusan motteru toki ni, kyū ni ame ga futtekite .... Ashimoto o mirareta n da ne.

Ⓐ That's expensive! It's twice as much as normal.

Ⓑ Yeah… It suddenly started raining when I had a lot of baggage, and so… I got taken advantage of.

★ **(~ no) 2 bai** = double ~, twice as many

J Assessing people, describing people as a certain type

K To be busy or flustered while acting

L To be nervous, to be worried

M Differences

N Encouraging someone

O Dealing with a situation sternly, dealing with a situation gently

P Taking criticism, blame, or an attack

Q Arrogant, proud, or stubborn attitudes

R To not match, to become weary, to be fed up

100 井の中の蛙
い　なか　かわず
I no naka no kawazu

Frog in a well

To become proud of one's position in a small world and unaware of the fact that a larger world exists. *Kawazu* is the old Japanese word for frog.

Listen & Speak

1 **Ⓐ** 優勝おめでとう。次はオリンピックだね。
ゆうしょう　　　　　　つぎ
Yūshō omedetō. Tsugi wa orinpikku da ne.

Ⓑ いえいえ、僕なんか、国内の試合しか知らない井の中の蛙
ぼく　　　　こくない　しあい　し　　　　い　なか　かわず
ですよ。
Ieie, boku nanka, kokunai no shiai shika shiranai i no naka no kawazu desu yo.

- **Ⓐ** Congratulations on the victory. Next up must be the Olympics.
- **Ⓑ** No, not at all. I'm just a frog in a well who has only ever tasted domestic victory.

★ *kokunai no* = domestic, home

2 **Ⓐ** どうして留学しようと思ったんですか。
りゅうがく　　　　おも
Dōshite ryūgaku shiyō to omotta n desu ka.

Ⓑ 結局は井の中の蛙だと思って……。自分の知らない世界を
けっきょく　い　なか　かわず　　　おも　　　　　じぶん　し　　　せかい
見たいと思ったんです。
み　　　　おも
Kekkyoku wa i no naka no kawazu da to omotte .... Jibun no shiranai sekai o mitai to omotta n desu.

- **Ⓐ** Why did you want to study abroad?
- **Ⓑ** Because I felt that I was just a frog in a well... I felt like I wanted to see a world I didn't know about.

★ *kekkyoku* = after all, finally

101 甘い汁を吸う
Amai shiru o sū

Skim off the cream

To use others for easy personal profit.

Listen & Speak

1 Ⓐ世の中厳しくなってきたから、彼らも今までみたいに<u>甘い汁を吸えなくなる</u>よ。

Yononaka kibishiku natte kita kara, karera mo ima made mitai ni amai shiru o suenaku naru yo.

Ⓑそうだよね。

Sō da yo ne.

Ⓐ The world has gotten tougher, so they can't skim off the cream like they used to be able to.

Ⓑ You're right.

★ *kibishī* = severe, tough

---

2 Ⓐこんなに安く仕入れて高く売ってるんだ！　結構<u>甘い汁吸ってる</u>んじゃない？

Konna ni yasuku shiirete takaku utteru n da! Kekkō amai shiru sutteru n ja nai?

Ⓑそんなことないよ。いろいろ費用がかかるから。

Sonna koto nai yo. Iroiro hiyō ga kakaru kara.

Ⓐ They're buying their stock for this cheap and selling it for so much! Aren't they just taking advantage? Skimming off the cream.

Ⓑ That's not true. There are a lot of costs involved.

★ *shiireru* = lay in a stock, buy in

102 目のかたきにする　Hold a grudge against
め

Me no kataki ni suru

To hate someone and see them in a hostile light.

Listen & Speak

1 Ⓐ 彼女はいつも私のこと、目の敵にするんだよね。
かのじょ　　　　わたし　　　　　め　かたき

Kanojo wa itsumo watashi no koto, me no kataki ni suru n da yo ne.

Ⓑ そうなの？　いやだね。

Sō na no? Iyada ne.

Ⓐ She always has a grudge against me.
Ⓑ Really? That's awful.

★ **iya (na)** =
unpleasant, nasty

2 Ⓐ また、店長に何か言われた？
てんちょう　なん　い

Mata, tenchō ni nanka iwareta?

Ⓑ そう。なんで私ばかり目の敵にされるのか、わからないよ。
わたし　　　　め　かたき

Sō. Nande watashi bakari me no kataki ni sareru no ka,

wakaranai yo.

Ⓐ Did the manager say something to you again?
Ⓑ Yes. I don't know why he has such a grudge against me specifically.

★ **X bakari ~** = always
~ X

置く　to put
お

Useful One-word Expressions in Japanese 27

1. To leave a gap in time or space　2. To leave something as it is

Ex.1) あの人と距離を置きたい。／３日置いて連絡した。
ひと　きょり　お　　　　　か　お　れんらく

I want to keep him at a distance. / I contacted him after three days.

Ex.2) その問題はしばらく置いておいてください。
もんだい　　　　お

Please put that problem to one side for the time being.

J Assessing people, describing people as a certain type

K To be busy or flustered while acting

L To be nervous, to be worried

M Differences

N Encouraging someone

O Dealing with a situation sternly, dealing with a situation gently

P Taking criticism, blame, or an attack

Q Arrogant, proud, or stubborn attitudes

R To not match, to become weary, to be fed up

103 水と油
みず あぶら
Mizu to abura

Water and oil; chalk and cheese; incompatible

To not mix well and to harmonize poorly.

Listen & Speak

1 Ⓐあの二人は水と油だよね。森さんは無口で、林さんはすごいおしゃべりだから。

Ano futari wa mizu to abura da yo ne. Mori-san wa mukuchi de, Hayashi-san wa sugoi oshaberi da kara.

Ⓑそうだね。

Sō da ne.

Ⓐ Those two are like water and oil. Mori-san is quiet, while Hayashi-san talks all the time.

Ⓑ You're right.

★ *mukuchi (na)* = very quiet, do not talk

---

2 Ⓐどうしたの？ 困った顔して。

Dōshita no? Komatta kao shite.

Ⓑうん。新しく入った人とどうも合わなくて……。完全に水と油って感じ。

Un. Atarashiku haitta hito to dōmo awanakute.... Kanzen ni mizu to abura tte kanji.

Ⓐ What's the matter? Why the troubled expression?

Ⓑ Well, I just can't get along with the new guy... It's like we're totally chalk and cheese.

★ *awanai* = not match, not get along with each other well

---

104 犬猿の仲
けんえん なか
Ken'en no naka

Like dogs and monkeys;
like cats and dogs

To have an extremely bad relationship,
like dogs and monkeys.

1 ❶ 昨日は珍しく田中さんとお昼を食べたんです。
きのう めずら たなか ひる た
Kinō wa mezurashiku Tanaka-san to ohiru o tabeta n desu.

❷ そうなんだ。でも、そのこと、彼に言わないほうがいいよ。
かれ い
あの二人、犬猿の仲だから。
ふたり けんえん なか
*Sō nan da. Demo, sono koto, kare ni iwanai hō ga ī yo. Ano
futari, ken'en no naka da kara.*

❶ I had lunch with Tanaka-san for once
yesterday.

❷ Really. Well, you shouldn't tell him that.
Those two are like cats and dogs.

★ *mezurashiku* = unusually

2 ❶ 林さんと森さんって、仲がいいと思ってたんですけど、本
はやし もり なか おも ほん
当は犬猿の仲なんですってね。
とう けんえん なか
*Hayashi-san to Mori-san tte, naka ga ī to omotteta n desu kedo,
hontō wa ken'en no naka nan desutte ne.*

❷ そうなんだよ。
Sō nan da yo.

❶ I thought Hayashi-san and Mori-san got
along, but they're actually like cats and
dogs, aren't they?

❷ Yes, they are.

★ *naka ga ī* = close, get along

123

J Assessing people, describing people as a certain type

K To be busy or flustered while acting

Q To be nervous, to be worried

M Differences

N Encouraging someone

O Dealing with a situation sternly, dealing with a situation gently

P Taking criticism, blame, or an attack

Q Arrogant, proud, or stubborn attitudes

R To not match, to become weary, to be fed up

105 アレルギー

Arerugī

Allergy; rejection

Used to indicate something one dislikes because of an excessive reaction they have to it. The expression is frequently used prior to something one dislikes, such as 「卵アレルギー」, 「猫アレルギー」, and 「金属アレルギー」.

Listen & Speak

1 Ⓐ 中学の時からずっと英語アレルギーだったんです。

Chūgaku no toki kara zutto ēgo arerugī datta n desu.

Ⓑ そうですか。何とかそのアレルギーを直しましょうね。

Sō desu ka. Nantoka sono arerugī o naoshimashō ne.

Ⓐ I've had an English allergy ever since I was in middle school.

Ⓑ Really. We need to do something to fix that.

★ ***arerugī*** = alergy

---

2 Ⓐ どうしたの？ 心配そうな顔して。

Dōshita no? Shinpai sōna kao shite.

Ⓑ だって、満員電車に乗るんでしょ？ 私、人混みアレルギーだから。

Datte, man'in densha ni noru n desho? Watashi, hitogomi arerugī dakara.

Ⓐ What's the matter? Why do you look so worried?

Ⓑ Well, we're going to get on a full train, aren't we? I'm allergic to crowded spaces.

★ ***hitogomi*** = crowd (of people)

---

106 耳にタコができる — Get an earache
Mimi ni tako ga dekiru

To be annoyed at being told something multiple times. A metaphor for one's ear developing a callous after hearing the same thing over and over, like one may develop a callous on their hand from writing with a pen too much.

1 ⓐ子供のころから「お父さんを追い越せ」って、<u>耳にタコができる</u>ほど言われてきたんです。

Kodomo no koro kara "otōsan o oikose" tte, mimi ni tako ga dekiru hodo iwaretekita n desu.

ⓑそれは負担だったでしょうね。

Sore wa futan datta deshō ne.

ⓐ I've been told that I need to overtake my father ever since I was a child to the point that it gives me an earache.

ⓑ That must have been a burden on you.

★ *oikosu* = overtake, pass
★ *futan* = burden, load

2 ⓐかぎ、全部閉めてきた？

Kagi, zenbu shimetekita?

ⓑもちろん。<u>耳にタコができる</u>ぐらい言われたからね。

Mochiron. Mimi ni tako ga dekiru gurai iwareta kara ne.

ⓐ Did you lock all the locks?

ⓑ Of course. You told me so many times it gave me an earache.

★ *zenbu* = all, whole, every

CD 54

107 鼻につく
はな
Hana ni tsuku

Get sick of

To grow to dislike something due to repetition. Comes from the idea of becoming annoyed at having to smell something time and time again.

Listen & Speak

1 Ⓐ 彼は確かにスピーチ上手だけど、いつもいつも同じ内容で鼻についてきたよ。

Kare wa tashika ni supīchi jōzu da kedo, itsumo itsumo onaji naiyō de hana ni tsuitekita yo.

Ⓑ そうだね。

Sō da ne.

Ⓐ He is good at giving speeches, but he always says the same thing, and I've gotten sick of it.

Ⓑ You're right.

★ **tashika ni** = definitely, certainly

---

2 Ⓐ あの人はいつも自分の自慢ばかり。

Ano hito wa itsumo jibun no jiman bakari.

Ⓑ そうですね。ちょっと鼻につきますね。

Sō desu ne. Chotto hana ni tsukimasu ne.

Ⓐ She's always bragging about herself.

Ⓑ You're right. You get kind of sick of it, don't you?

★ **jiman** = boast

---

108 大きなお世話
Ōkina o-sewa

Mind your own business

To reject assistance offered by someone because you are unable to straightforwardly accept it.

Listen & Speak

1 Ⓐ田中さんが「早く結婚したほうがいいよ」だって。
Tanaka-san ga "hayaku kekkon shita hō ga ī yo" da tte.

Ⓑ親切な人だけど、<u>大きなお世話</u>だよね。
Shinsetsuna hito da kedo, ōkina osewa da yo ne.

Ⓐ Tanaka-san says "You ought to get married soon."

Ⓑ She's a nice person, but she needs to mind her own business.

★ **~ da tte** = I hear ~, He/She said ~, They say ~

2 Ⓐ早く寝たほうがやせるのにもいいらしいよ。
Hayaku neta hō ga yaseru no nimo ī rashī yo.

Ⓑ<u>大きなお世話</u>です。ほっといてください。
Ōkina o-sewa desu. Hottoite kudasai.

Ⓐ I heard going to sleep early helps you lose weight, too.

Ⓑ Mind your own business. Leave me alone.

★ **yaseru** = lose weight

口 mouth
くち

Useful One-word Expressions in Japanese 28

1. Somewhere people and things go in and out of 2.the number of times one eats or drinks 3. Ability of speech 4. The way of saying something

Ex.1) 入口／駅の北口／ビンの口
いりぐち／えきのきたぐち／ビンのくち
Entrance / the north exit of a station / the mouth of a bottle

Ex.2) 一口食べる
ひとくちたべる
To eat one mouthful

Ex.3) 彼は口がうまい。
かれはくちがうまい。
He's an articulate speaker.

Ex.4) 彼は口が悪い。
かれはくちがわるい。
He says unkind things.

Ⓙ Assessing people, describing people as a certain type

Ⓚ To be busy or flustered while acting

Ⓠ To be nervous, to be worried

Ⓜ Differences

Ⓝ Encouraging someone

Ⓞ Dealing with a situation sternly, dealing with a situation gently

Ⓟ Taking criticism, blame, or an attack

Ⓠ Arrogant, proud, or stubborn attitudes

Ⓡ To not match, to become weary, to be fed up

109 開いた口がふさがらない

Aita kuchi ga fusagaranai

Jaw hit the floor; astonished

To be incredibly shocked, to the point that one is so dumbfounded they forget to even close their open mouth.

Listen & Speak

1 Ⓐ「働かせてください」って頭下げて頼んだくせに、３日で やめて、「３日分の給料ください」だって。開いた口がふ さがらなかったよ。

"Hatarakasete kudasai" tte atama sagete tanonda kuse ni, mikka de yamete, "mikka-bun no kyūrō kudasai" da tte. Aita kuchi ga fusagaranakatta yo.

Ⓑひどい人がいるねえ。

Hidoi hito ga iru nē.

Ⓐ He begged us to let him work here, but he quit after three days and asked for three days' worth of pay. My jaw hit the floor.

Ⓑ There are some awful people out there.

★ **atama o sageru** = apologize

★ **hidoi** = awful, terrible

2 Ⓐこれ見て。花屋に花束頼んだら、しおれた古い花入れてき たよ。

Kore mite. Hana-ya ni hanataba tanondara, sioreta furui hana irete kita yo.

Ⓑひどいなあ。開いた口がふさがらないね。

Hidoinā. Aita kuchi ga fusagaranai ne.

Ⓐ Look at this. I ordered a bouquet from a florist, but it had these old and wilted flowers in it.

Ⓑ That's awful. Your jaw must have hit the floor.

★ **hanataba** = bouquet

★ **shioreta** = wilted

110 手に負えない
Te ni oenai

More than I can handle

For something to be beyond one's ability to handle. A situation beyond one's capacities.

J Assessing people, describing people as a certain type

K To be busy or flustered while acting

Q To be nervous, to be worried

M Differences

N Encouraging someone

O Dealing with a situation, steering, dealing with a situation gently

P Taking criticism, blame, or an attack

Q Arrogant, proud, or stubborn attitudes

R To not match, to become weary, to be fed up

Listen & Speak

1 Ⓐ〈子供たちの世話〉

いやー、みんな元気がよすぎて、手に負えないよ。

〈Kodomo-tachi no sewa〉

Iyā, minna genki ga yosugite, te ni oenai yo.

Ⓑ ご苦労様でした。あとは私がやりますので。

Gokurō-sama deshita. Ato wa watashi ga yarimasu node.

Ⓐ (Taking care of children) Oh, they're all so energetic that they were more than I can handle.

Ⓑ Thank you for your work. I'll take care of the rest.

★ **genki ga ī** = energetic, brisky

2 Ⓐ パソコン、どう？　直った？

Pasokon, dō? Naotta?

Ⓑ いや、全然だめ。僕の手に負えない感じ。

Iya, zenzen dame. Boku no te ni oenai kanji.

Ⓐ How is your computer? Is it fixed?

Ⓑ No, it's no good at all. It's more than I can handle on my own.

★ **naoru** = be mended, be restored

3 負ける　to lose, be defeated　**Useful One-word Expressions in Japanese**

To lower a price

Ex.) 1000 円負ける／もう少し負けてもらえませんか。

To reduce a price by ¥1,000 / Can't you lower the price a bit more?

111 手につかない
て
Te ni tsukanai

Can't bring myself to

To feel uninterested in doing anything. To be unable to give one's attention to anything else because of a worrying or pressing matter.

Listen & Speak

1 Ⓐ どうしたの？ぼーっとして。

Dō shita no ? Bōtto shite.

Ⓑ すみません。病院の検査結果が気になって、仕事が<u>手につ</u>
びょういん けんさ けっか き しごと て
<u>かない</u>んです。

Sumimasen. Byōin no kensa-kekka ga ki ni natte, shigoto ga te ni tsukanai n desu.

Ⓐ What's the matter? You're spaced out.
Ⓑ I'm sorry. I'm worried about my hospital test results and I can't bring myself to do any work.

★ *kensa* = inspection, checkup

2 Ⓐ 彼、元気ないね。
かれ げんき
Kare, genki nai ne.

Ⓑ 試験に落ちたのがショックで、何も<u>手につかない</u>みたい。
しけん お なに て
Shiken ni ochita no ga shokku de, nani mo te ni tsukanai mitai.

Ⓐ He's very unenergetic.
Ⓑ He's shocked that he failed his test, and he can't seem to bring himself to do anything.

★ *shiken ni ochiru* = fail an examination

112 心ここにあらず
こころ
Kokoro koko ni arazu

Heart is somewhere else

To be occupied with something and
unable to focus on what is in front of you.

S Dazed, unfocused, unenthusiastic

T Having a problem, undesired situations or results, tight situations

U To be embarrassed, to be reflective

V To endure, to withstand difficulty, to make a sacrifice, to take a risk

W To be extremely surprised, to feel fear

X Suffering a mishap, being betrayed, something going wrong

Y Doing well and poorly, conditions going well and poorly

Z Other

INDEX

Listen & Speak

1

Ⓐ ここ一週間ぐらい、ずっと心ここにあらず、って感じだね。
いっしゅうかん こころ かん
Koko isshūkan gurai, zutto kokoro koko ni arazu, tte kanji da ne.

Ⓑ すみません、ちょっと心配なことがあって。
しんぱい
Sumimasen, chotto shinpaina koto ga atte.

> Ⓐ It's like your heart has been somewhere
> else for about a week now.
> Ⓑ I'm sorry, there's something that has
> been worrying me a little bit.

> ★ *shinpaina koto ga aru*
> = have something to warry
> about

2

Ⓐ 彼女、もうすぐ結婚するんだって？
かのじょ けっこん
Kanojo, mōsugu kekkon suru n da tte?

Ⓑ 今週の土曜日。だから、会社でも心ここにあらずって感じ
こんしゅう どようび かいしゃ こころ かん
ね。

*Konshū no doyōbi. Dakara, kaisha demo kokoro koko ni arazu tte
kanji ne.*

> Ⓐ I heard she's going to get married soon?
> Ⓑ This Saturday. So it seems like her heart
> is somewhere else, even at work.

> ★ *mōsugu* = soon

113 **身が入らない**
Mi ga hairanai

Can't put yourself into it

To be unable to seriously apply oneself to something because of a concern or lack of interest.

Listen & Speak

1 Ⓐなんだかいつもと違うね。どうしたの？

Nandaka itsumo to chigau ne. Dō shita no?

Ⓑうん、いろいろあって、練習に<u>身が入らない</u>んだ。

Un, iroiro atte, renshū ni mi ga hairanai n da.

- Ⓐ Something about you seems different. What's the matter?
- Ⓑ Well, a lot happened and I can't put myself into practice.

★ ***itsumo to chigau*** = different from usual

2 Ⓐゲームばかりして、勉強に<u>身が入ってない</u>んじゃない？

Gēmu bakari shite, benkyō ni mi ga haittenai n ja nai?

Ⓑそんなことないですよ。

Sonna koto nai desu yo.

- Ⓐ Aren't you playing games all the time and not putting yourself into your studies?
- Ⓑ That's not true.

★ ***sonna koto nai*** = not at all, I don't think so

気 mind
き

Useful One-word Expressions in Japanese **30**

1. Worry, care   2. Mood, feeling   3. Will, intention   4. Consciousness

Ex.1) 気になる／気をつける
き　　　　き
To worry / to be careful

Ex.3) やる気はある／負ける気がしない
き　　　　　　ま　　　き
To be motivated / I don't think I will lose.

Ex.2) 気が楽だ。／気が重い。
き　らく　　　き　おも
Relieved, calm. / depressed

Ex.4) 気を失う／気が遠くなる
き　うしな　き　とお
To lose consciousness / To faint

132

114 煮え切らない
Niekiranai
(に) (き)

Halfhearted

To not have a focused attitude. To be fairly unable to make a decision.

1 Ⓐ 彼、ずっと転職したいって言ってたから、いい所を紹介したのに、なんか煮え切らないんだよな。
_{かれ てんしょく い ところ しょうかい に き}

Kare, zutto tensyoku shitai tte itteta kara, ī tokoro o shōkai shita noni, nanka niekiranai n da yo na.

Ⓑ そうなんですか。

Sō na n desu ka?

Ⓐ He's always been saying that he wants to change jobs, so I introduced him to a good place, but he seems to be halfhearted about it.

Ⓑ Is that so?

★ ***tenshoku suru*** = change one's job

---

2 Ⓐ ええ……まあ、やることはやりますが……はい。

Eē ... mā, yaru koto wa yarimasu ga...hai.

Ⓑ そんな煮え切らない態度じゃ、困るよ。
_{に き たいど こま}

Sonna niekiranai taido ja, komaru yo.

Ⓐ What…? Well, I'll do what I need to do… Okay.

Ⓑ I can't have you taking such a halfhearted attitude.

★ ***taido*** = attitude

CD 58

115 ネックになる

Bottlenecked

Nekku ni naru

For things to become obstructed. 「ネック」 is not in reference to a human neck but to the neck of a bottle. As this section is narrow, one cannot smoothly put things inside it.

Listen & Speak

1 Ⓐ いい店なのに、場所が<u>ネックになってる</u>よね。

Ī mise nanoni, basho ga nekku ni natteru yo ne.

Ⓑ うん。この辺、全然人が通らないもの。

Un. Kono hen, zenzen hito ga tōranai mono.

Ⓐ It's a good store, but the location is a bottleneck.

Ⓑ Yes. People don't pass by this area at all.

★ **tōru** = passs

2 Ⓐ 会社をつくる話、どうなった？

Kaisha o tsukuru hanashi, dō natta?

Ⓑ それが、資金不足が<u>ネックになって</u>、進んでないんです。

Sore ga, shikin-busoku ga nekku ni natte, susundenai n desu.

Ⓐ What happened to that talk of forming a company?

Ⓑ Well, it's not moving forward because a lack of capital is causing a bottleneck.

★ **shikin** = fund
★ **fusoku** = lack, shortage

S Dazed, unfocused, unenthusiastic

T Having a problem, undesired situations or results, tight situations

U To be embarrassed, to be reflective

V To endure, to withstand difficulty, to make a sacrifice, to take a risk

W To be extremely surprised, to feel fear

X Suffering a mishap, being betrayed, something going wrong

Y Doing well and poorly, conditions going well and poorly

Z Other

INDEX

116 壁にぶつかる
かべ
Kabe ni butsukaru

To hit a wall

To have to directly face a hard-to-solve problem. 「ぶちあたる」is also often used instead of 「ぶつかる」.

1 Ⓐ 最後の最後でこんな壁にぶつかるなんて、思ってもみな
さいご さいご かべ おも
かったよ。

Saigo no saigo de konna kabe ni butsukaru nante, omotte mo minakatta yo.

Ⓑ そうですね。困りましたね。
こま

Sō desu ne. Komarimashita ne.

Ⓐ I never imagined we would hit a wall like this at the very end of everything.

Ⓑ You're right. What a problem.

★ **saigo** = last

2 Ⓐ 山下、最近、調子悪いね。何か壁にぶつかってるんだろうね。
やました さいきん ちょうし わる なに かべ

Yamashita, saikin, chōshi warui ne. Nanika kabe ni butsukatteru n darō ne.

Ⓑ そうだね。でも、彼ならきっと乗り越えられるよ。
かれ の こ

Sō da ne. Demo, kare nara kitto norikoerareru yo.

Ⓐ Yamashita hasn't been doing well recently. I wonder if he has run up against some kind of wall.

Ⓑ I agree. But knowing him, I'm sure he can get over it.

★ **chōshi ga warui** = out of form

★ **norikoeru** = get over

117 # お手上げ
<ruby>て</ruby> <ruby>あ</ruby>
Oteage

To throw up one's hands

To be in a hopeless situation. To be at one's limits and unable to do anything. Comes from the pose of holding both hands up and surrendering.

Listen & Speak

1 Ⓐ テストどうだった？

Tesuto dōdatta?

Ⓑ もう<u>お手上げ</u>。全然ヤマがはずれちゃった。
<ruby>て</ruby> <ruby>あ</ruby> <ruby>ぜんぜん</ruby>

Mō oteage. Zenzen yama ga hazurechatta.

Ⓐ How was the test?
Ⓑ I threw up my hands. I guessed completely wrong about what would be on it.

★ *yama ga hazureru* = guess wrong

2 Ⓐ 旅先でパスポート取られたら、<u>お手上げ</u>ですから、失くさないように気をつけてくださいね。
<ruby>たびさき</ruby> <ruby>と</ruby> <ruby>て</ruby> <ruby>あ</ruby> <ruby>な</ruby> <ruby>き</ruby>

Tabisaki de pasupōto toraretara, oteage desu kara, nakusanai yō ni ki o tsukete kudasai ne.

Ⓑ はい。

Hai.

Ⓐ You'll be forced to throw up your hands if your passport is stolen while on your trip, so be careful not to lose it.
Ⓑ Okay.

★ *tabisaki de* = while traveling

118 手も足も出ない
Te mo ashi mo denai

Can't do a thing

To have no plan one can follow. To be in a hopeless situation. 「手」
and 「足」 refer to methods and plans.

Listen & Speak

1 **Ⓐ** 弁護士と一緒に行ったら、相手は<u>手も足も出ない</u>って感じだったよ。

Bengoshi to issho ni ittara, aite wa te mo ashi mo denai tte kanji datta yo.

Ⓑ それはそうでしょう。法律の専門家だもの。

Sore wa sō deshō. Hōristu no senmonka da mono.

Ⓐ I went with a lawyer andit seemed like the other guys couldn't do a thing.

Ⓑ Of course. You were with a legal expert.

★ ***bengoshi*** = lawyer
★ ***senmonka*** = specialist

2 **Ⓐ** 試験、どんな問題だった？

Shiken, donna mondai datta?

Ⓑ もう<u>手も足も出なかった</u>よ。問題の意味もわからなかった。

Mō te mo ashi mo denakatta yo. Mondai no imi mo wakaranakatta.

Ⓐ What kind of questions were on the test?

Ⓑ I couldn't do a thing about it. I didn't even understand what the questions meant.

★ ***imi*** = meaning

おいしい delicious

Useful One-word Expressions in Japanese

Suits oneself, is favourable to oneself

Ex.) おいしい話には気をつけたほうがいい。／おいしい仕事を見つけた。
You should be careful of tempting offers. / I found a great job.

119 板ばさみ
いた
Ita basami

Between a rock and a hard place

To stand between two opposing forces and be in the difficult position of being unable to choose either one. From the situation of being stuck between two planks and unable to move.

Listen & Speak

1 Ⓐ 疲れた顔してるね。
つか　かお
Tsukareta kao shiteru ne.

Ⓑ わかる？ 部長と課長の<u>板ばさみ</u>で大変なんだよ、今。
ぶちょう　かちょう　　　いた　　　　たいへん　　　　　いま
Wakaru? Buchō to kachō no itabasami de taihen na n da yo, ima.

Ⓐ You look tired.

Ⓑ You could tell? I'm stuck between a rock and a hard place with the division chief and the section chief right now.

★ **tsukareta** = weary, tired

2 Ⓐ 母さん、ごめんね、。いつも僕と父さんとの<u>板ばさみ</u>で困
かあ　　　　　　　　　　　　ぼく　ちち　　　　　いた　　　　　こま
らせちゃって。

Kāsan, gomen ne. Itsumo boku to tōsan to no itabasami de komarasechatte.

Ⓑ しょうがないよ。

Shōganai yo.

Ⓐ Sorry, Mom. You're always stuck between a rock and a hard place with me and Dad.

Ⓑ There's no helping it.

★ **komaraseru** = cause someone trouble, annoy someone

120

裏目に出る
うら め で
Backfire

Urame ni deru

To expect a good result but to get an unfavourable one instead.

Listen & Speak

1 Ⓐ 親切のつもりでしたことが裏目に出ちゃった。
しんせつ うら め で

Shinsetsu no tsumori de shita koto ga urame ni dechatta.

Ⓑ それで恨まれるの？ かわいそうに。
うら

Sore de uramareru no? Kawaisō ni.

Ⓐ I thought I was being kind but it backfired.

Ⓑ And he resents you because of that? You poor thing.

★ *uramu (≒ waruku omou)* = think ill of

2 Ⓐ えっ、これ全部枯らしちゃったの？
ぜん ぶ か

Ett, kore zenbu karashichatta no?

Ⓑ そう。水をたくさんあげたのが裏目に出ちゃって。
みず うら め で

Sō. Mizu o takusan ageta no ga urame ni dechatte.

Ⓐ What, these all withered?

Ⓑ Yes. I gave them a lot of water but it backfired.

★ *karasu* = blight, let die

お茶 tea
ちゃ

Useful One-word Expressions in Japanese **32**

1. Soft drinks such as tea and coffee, but excluding green tea

2. To take a break

Ex.1) どこかでお茶を飲みましょう。　Ex.2) そろそろお茶にしませんか。
ちゃ の ちゃ

Let's have tea somewhere.　　　　　　Would you like to take a break soon?

Ⓢ Dazed, unfocused, unenthusiastic

Ⓣ Having a problem, undesired situations or results, tight situations

Ⓤ To be embarrassed, difficulty, to make a sacrifice, to take a risk, to be reflective

Ⓥ To endure, to withstand, difficulty, to make a sacrifice, to take a risk

Ⓦ To be extremely surprised, to feel fear

Ⓧ Suffering, a mishap, being betrayed, something going wrong

Ⓨ Doing well and poorly, conditions going well and poorly

Ⓩ Other

INDEX

121 頭が痛い
あたま いた
Atama ga itai

Get a headache

To suffer and be troubled by something that one cannot solve.

1 Ⓐ娘の結婚のことで<u>頭が痛い</u>よ、ほんとに。
むすめ けっこん あたま いた

Musume no kekkon no koto de atama ga itai yo, honto ni.

Ⓑ大変ですね。
たいへん

Taihen desu ne.

Ⓐ My daughter's marriage is really giving me a headache.

Ⓑ It must be hard.

★ ***taihen (na)*** = tough, difficult, hard

2 Ⓐ消費税がまた上がるらしいよ。
しょう ひ ぜい あ

Shōhizē ga mata agaru rashī yo.

Ⓑまたー!? 今でも大変なのに、ますます<u>頭が痛く</u>なりそう。
いま たいへん あたま いた

Matā!? Ima demo taihen na noni, masumasu atama ga itaku nari sō.

Ⓐ It sounds like the sales tax is going up again.

Ⓑ Again?! It's already hard enough, this feels like it's only going to be a bigger headache.

★ ***shōhizē*** = consumption tax

---

 sweet
あま

 Useful One-word Expressions in Japanese

1. Lacking severity, not reliable, immature   2. To trick someone
3. Feeling of rapture

Ex.1) 甘い計画／自分に甘い
あま けいかく じ ぶん あま
A badly thought out plan / self- indulgent

Ex.2) 甘い言葉で誘う
あま こと ば さそ
To lead someone on with sweet talk

Ex.3) 甘い思い出
あま おも で
Sweet memories

122 心が折れる
こころ お
Kokoro ga oreru

Heart is crushed; to have one's heart broken

To lose one's emotional support and feel dispirited. To lose one's ambition.

1 Ⓐ 彼、クラブやめるって。
かれ
Kare, kurabu yameru tte.

Ⓑ そうか。けがをしてから、心が折れたような感じだったからね。
こころ お かん

Sō ka. Kega o shite kara, kokoro ga oreta yō na kanji datta kara ne.

Ⓐ It sounds like he's quitting the club.
Ⓑ Oh. It did feel like his heart was crushed after getting injured.

★ *kega o suru* = get injured

2 Ⓐ 部長、ひどいこと言うね。
ぶ ちょう い
Buchō, hidoi koto yū ne.

Ⓑ ほんと。あんなふうに言われたら、心が折れるよ。
い こころ お

Honto. Anna fū ni iwaretara, kokoro ga oreru yo.

Ⓐ The department chief says the meanest things.
Ⓑ He really does. Having those kinds of things said to you can really bring you down

★ *hidoi koto o iu(yū)* = say nasty things

123 死にそう
し
Shinisō

About to die; feel like dying

To be in a difficult situation and unable to do anything.

Listen & Speak

1 Ⓐあともうちょっとで着くから。
う
Ato mō chotto de tsuku kara.

Ⓑうん……。お腹すいて死にそう。
なか　　し
Un.... onaka suite shinisō.

Ⓐ I'll be there in just a bit more.
Ⓑ Okay... I'm so hungry I'm about to die.

★ **onaka ga suku** = become hungry

2 Ⓐ……じゃ、来週はどうですか。
らいしゅう
....Ja. raishū wa dō desu ka?

Ⓑ来週もだめです。今月はもう死にそうに忙しいんです。
らいしゅう　　　　こんげつ　　　　し　　　　　いそが
Raishū mo dame desu. Kongetsu wa mō shinisō ni isogashī n desu.

Ⓐ ...Then how is next week?
Ⓑ Next week isn't any good either. I'm so busy this month that I'm about to die.

★ **dame (na)** = not good, impossible

飲む・のむ to drink　**Useful One-word Expressions in Japanese**
の

I. To drink alcohol　2. To accept a compromise

Ex.I) これから飲みに行きませんか。／飲み会
の　　い　　　　　　　　　　　　の　かい
／飲み過ぎに注意してください。
の　す　　　ちゅうい
Would you like to go out for a drink now? / A drinks party
/ Please be careful not to drink too much.

Ex.2) その条件をのんだ。
じょうけん
He accepted the conditions.

124 煮詰まる

Reach an impasse

Nitsumaru

To reach one's limits. Originally used in a positive sense to describe a state where a conclusion is close at hand, but recently it is often used in a negative sense to mean "to reach one's limits."

1 Ⓐいい方法がないか、一生懸命考えてるんだけど、<u>煮詰まっちゃって</u>。
ほうほう　　　　　　　いっしょうけんめいかんが　　　　　　　　　　　　　　につ

Ī hōhō ga nai ka, isshōkenmē kangaeteru n da kedo, nitsumacchatte.

Ⓑ少し休んだら？
すこ　やす

Sukoshi yasundara?

Ⓐ I racked my brain to come up with a good method, but I reached an impasse.

Ⓑ Why don't you take a little break?

★ **isshōkenmē** = for one's life, with all one's might

---

2 Ⓐ会議、ずいぶん長いね。まだ終わらないの？
かいぎ　　　　　　なが　　　　　　　お

Kaigi, zuibun nagai ne. Mada owaranai no?

Ⓑ意見がなかなかまとまらなくて、<u>煮詰まってる</u>みたいよ。
いけん　　　　　　　　　　　　　　　　　につ

Iken ga nakanaka matomaranakute, nitsumatteru mitai yo.

Ⓐ The meeting's taking quite a long time. Is it still not over?

Ⓑ They can't reach an agreement and it seems like they've got stuck.

★ **matomaru** = be settled, reach an agreement

Ⓢ Dazed, unfocused, unenthusiastic

Ⓣ Having a problem, undesired situations or results, tight situations

Ⓤ To be embarrassed, to be reflective

Ⓥ To undergo difficulty, to withstand, to make a sacrifice, to take a risk

Ⓦ To be extremely surprised, to feel fear!

Ⓧ Suffering a mistake, being betrayed, something going wrong

Ⓨ Doing well and poorly, conditions going well and poorly

Ⓩ Other

INDEX

CD 63

125 顔から火が出る
かお ひ で
Kao kara hi ga deru

Burn with shame

When one's face grows flushed and red out of embarrassment. Often followed by 「～ほど恥ずかしい」. A metaphor for one's face growing so red it seems like it may catch on fire.

Listen & Speak

1 Ⓐ 大勢の前でこんな初歩的なミスをするなんて、<u>顔から火が出る</u>ほど恥ずかしかったよ。

Ōzē no mae de konna shohoteki na misu o suru nante, kao kara hi ga deru hodo hazukashikatta yo.

Ⓑ そんな。大したことないよ。

Sonna. Taishita koto nai yo.

Ⓐ I was burning with shame after making such a basic mistake in front of so many people.

Ⓑ What? It wasn't a big deal.

★ **shohoteki (na)** = elementary

2 Ⓐ けさ、電車の中で知らない人を田中先生と間違えて大声で呼んじゃったよ。<u>顔から火が出る</u>ほど恥ずかしかった！

Kesa, densha no naka de shiranai hito o Tanaka-sensē to machigaete ōgoe de yonjatta yo. Kao kara hi ga deru hodo hazukashikatta!

Ⓑ やっちゃったね。

Yacchatta ne.

Ⓐ On the train this morning, I mistook a complete stranger for Tanaka-sensei and called out to him in a loud voice. I was so embarrassed!

Ⓑ You really messed up there.

★ **ōgoe de** = aloud

144

126 穴があったら入りたい
あな　　　　　はい

Ana ga attara hairitai

Want to dig a hole and hide in it

To be so embarrassed one wants to hide because they find it difficult to stay in a location.

1 Ⓐ 今日ずっと、セール価格の値札つけたまま服着てたよ！
きょう　　　　　　　　　かかく　　ねふだ　　　　　　　ふく き
もう、恥ずかしくて穴があったら入りたいくらい！
は　　　　　　　　あな　　　　　　はい

Kyō zutto, sēru-kakaku no nefuda tsuketa mama fuku kiteta yo!
Mō, hazukashikute ana ga attara hairitai kurai!

Ⓑ 大丈夫だよ、誰も気づいてないって。
だいじょう ぶ　　　　だれ　き

Daijōbu da yo, dare mo kizuitenai tte.

Ⓐ I wore these clothes all day with the sale price tag still on them! Oh, I'm so embarrassed that I want to dig a hole and hide in it!

Ⓑ It's fine, no one noticed.

★ **sēru** = sale
★ **nefuda** = price tag

2 Ⓐ あー、穴があったら入りたいよ。彼に送るメール、先生に
あな　　　　　はい　　　　かれ　おく　　　　　せんせい
送っちゃった。名前が同じだから間違えちゃって。
おく　　　　　　　なまえ　おな　　　　　　まちが

Ā, ana ga attara hairitai yo. Kare ni okuru mēru, sensē ni okucchatta. Namae ga onaji da kara machigaechatte.

Ⓑ うそー！

Usō!

Ⓐ Ah, I want to dig a hole and hide in it. I sent an email meant for my boyfriend to our teacher instead. I made a mistake because they have the same name.

Ⓑ No way!

★ **onaji** = same

S Dazed, unfocused, unenthusiastic

T Having a problem, unsettled situations or results, tight situations

U To be embarrassed, to be reflective

V To endure, to withstand, difficulty, to make a sacrifice, to take a risk

W To be extremely surprised, to feel fear

X suffering & mishap, being betrayed, something going wrong

Y Doing well and poorly, conditions going well and poorly

Z Other

INDEX

127　耳が痛い

みみ が いた

Mimi ga itai

Hurts to hear

When something someone else says hits a personal weak point, making it difficult to hear.

1 Ⓐさっきの話、耳が痛かったよ。まるで自分のこと言われているみたいで。

Sakki no hanashi, mimi ga itakatta yo. Marude jibun no koto iwareteiru mitai de.

Ⓑえっ、全然そんなつもりで言ったんじゃなかったんだけど。

Ett, zenzen sonna tsumori de itta n ja nakatta n da kedo.

Ⓐ It hurt to hear that just now. It was like you were talking about me.

Ⓑ What? That's not what I meant to do at all.

★ **marude ~** = just like ~, as if ~

2 Ⓐ先生、今日のお話は私たち母親にはとても耳が痛い話でした。

Sensē, kyō no o-hanashi wa watashi-tachi hahaoya niwa totemo mimi ga itai hanashi deshita.

Ⓑいやいや、参考の一つにしてくだされば。

Iyaiya, sankō no hitotsu ni shite kudasareba.

Ⓐ Sensei, today's talk hurt us mothers a lot to hear.

Ⓑ No, no. Just see it as something to think about.

★ **sankō** = reference

S Dazed, unfocused, unenthusiastic

T Having a problem, undesired situations or results, tight situations

U To be embarrassed, to be reflective

V To endure, to withstand difficulty, to make a sacrifice, to take a risk

W To be extremely surprised, to feel fear

X Suffering a mishap, being betrayed, something going wrong

Y Doing well and poorly, conditions going well and poorly

Z Other

INDEX

128 合わせる顔がない　Can't show my face
あ　　　　かお

Awaseru kao ga nai

To feel so sorry that one cannot appear in front of someone else.

Listen & Speak

1

Ⓐ 田村先輩が来てるよ。
たむらせんぱい　き

Tamura-senpai ga kiteru yo.

Ⓑ そう……。でも、先輩との約束が果たせてないから、合わ
せんぱい　　やくそく　は　　　　　　　　　　　　あ
せる顔がないなあ。
かお

Sō.... Demo, senpai tono yakusoku ga hatasetenai kara, awaseru kao ga nai nā.

> **Ⓐ** Tamura-sempai is here.
>
> **Ⓑ** Oh… But I can't show my face to him, because I haven't been able to keep my promise with him.

★ *yakusoku* = promise

2

Ⓐ 不合格だったら、先生に合わせる顔がないよ。あんなに一
ふごうかく　　　　　　せんせい　あ　　　　かお　　　　　　　　　　　　いっ
生懸命教えてくれたから。
しょうけんめいおし

Fugōkaku dattara, sensē ni awaseru kao ga nai yo. Annani isshōkenmē oshiete kureta kara.

Ⓑ そんなことないよ。

Sonna koto nai yo.

> **Ⓐ** I can't show my face to sensei because I didn't pass. She worked so hard to teach us.
>
> **Ⓑ** That's not the case at all.

★ *fugōkaku* = fail, exam failure

129 大人げない
おとな
Otonage nai

Immature; childish

Something childish that lacks prudence and discretion.

Listen & Speak

1 **Ⓐ** 昨日はすみません、ついカッとなって。大人げなかったです。
きのう　　　　　　　　　　　　　　　　　　おとな

　　Kinō wa sumimasen, tsui katto natte. Otonage nakatta desu.

Ⓑ いいよ、わかれば。

　　Ī yo, wakareba.

Ⓐ I'm sorry about yesterday, I suddenly got upset. It was immature of me.

Ⓑ It's okay, as long as you understand.

★ **katto naru** = I ose temper, get mad

2 **Ⓐ** そんなの僕の責任じゃないよ。
　　　　　　ぼく　せきにん

　　Sonna no boku no sekinin ja nai yo.

Ⓑ そういう言い方はちょっと大人げないんじゃない？
　　　　　　い　かた　　　　　　おとな

　　Sōyū īkata wa chotto otonage nai n ja nai?

Ⓐ That's not my fault.

Ⓑ Don't you think it's a bit childish to say that?

★ **sekinin** = responsibility

胸 chest
むね

Useful One-word Expressions in Japanese **35**

I. Heart 2. "To borrow someone's chest" is an expression which originates in the world of sumo wrestling and means, "To practise a skill with somebody who is more expert than you". "To lend one's chest" means "to allow someone less skilled than you to practise on you."

Ex.1) 胸がいっぱいになる。
　　　　むね

To become emotional.

Ex.2) 明日の試合は、胸を借りるつもりで頑張ります。
　　　あした　しあい　　むね　か　　　　　　　　がんば

In tomorrow's match, the other team is stronger, but it will be good practice and I'll do my best.

130 頭を冷やす
あたま　ひ
Atama o hiyasu

Cool your head

To hold back one's excited emotions and become calm.

Listen & Speak

1 Ⓐ少しは頭を冷やしてよ。さっきから怒鳴ってばかりで、何
すこ　　あたま　ひ　　　　　　　　　　　ど　な　　　　　　　なに
言ってるか、よくわからないよ。
い

Sukoshi wa atama o hiyashite yo. Sakki kara donatte bakari de, nani itteru ka, yoku wakaranai yo.

Ⓑちゃんと聞いてないからだよ。
き

Chanto kītenai kara da yo.

Ⓐ Cool your head a bit. You've just been screaming for a while now, and I don't know what you're trying to say.
Ⓑ It's because you're not listening.

★ **donaru** = bawl, roar

2 Ⓐあれっ、店長、どこ行ったの？
てんちょう　　　い

Arett, tenchō, doko itta no?

Ⓑさっき電話で怒ってたから、頭冷やしに外、行ったんじゃ
でんわ　おこ　　　　　あたま　ひ　　　そと　い
ない？

Sakki denwa de okotteta kara, atama hiyashini soto, itta n ja nai?

Ⓐ Huh? Where did the manager go?
Ⓑ He got mad on the phone earlier, so he probably went outside to cool his head, right?

★ **soto ni iku (=soto ni deru)** = go out, go outside

131 肩身が狭い
かた み せま
Katami ga semai

Feeling small

To feel inferior compared to others, and to feel uncomfortable and small. 肩身 refers to one's body.
かた み

Listen & Speak

1 Ⓐ みんなはちゃんと参加代払って参加してるけど、私は払っ
さん か だいはら さん か わたし はら
てないから肩身が狭いよ。
かた み せま

*Minna wa chanto sanka-dai haratte sanka shiteru kedo, watashi
wa harattenai kara katami ga semai yo.*

Ⓑ そんなこと、気にしなくていいんじゃない？
き

Sonna koto, ki ni shinakute ī n ja nai?

Ⓐ Everyone participating has properly paid
the participation fee, but I feel small
because I haven't paid.

Ⓑ I don't think you need to worry about
that, do you?

★ **ki ni suru** = mind

2 Ⓐ 今日はずいぶん静かだね。
きょう しず

Kyō wa zuibun shizuka da ne.

Ⓑ だって、結婚している人ばかりで、僕だけ独身。肩身狭い
けっこん ひと ぼく どくしん かた み せま
から。

*Datte, kekkon shiteiru hito bakari de, boku dake dokushin.
Katami semai kara.*

Ⓐ You're pretty quiet today, aren't you?

Ⓑ Well, it's all married people, and I'm the
only single one. I feel awkward.

★ **zuibun** = awfully, quite,
considerably

★ **dokushin** = single

132 お騒がせする
さわ
O-sawagase suru

Cause trouble

To create disorder or worry in society or among those nearby.

Listen & Speak

1 Ⓐ このたびは、いろいろお騒がせして、本当に申し訳ありま
さわ ほんとう もう わけ
せんでした。

Konotabi wa, iroiro o-sawagase shite, hontō ni mōshiwake arimasen deshita.

Ⓑ 大変だったね、いろいろ。
たいへん
Taihen datta ne, iroiro.

> Ⓐ I'm truly sorry for having caused trouble.
>
> Ⓑ It all must have been very hard.

★ **kono tabi (wa)** = this time

2 Ⓐ どうしよう、こんなに大きな騒ぎになっちゃって。
おお さわ
Dō shiyō, konna ni ōkina sawagi ni nacchatte.

Ⓑ 「お騒がせして申し訳ありませんでした」って、一度みん
さわ もう わけ いち ど
なに謝っといたほうがいいんじゃない？
あやま
"o-sawagase shite mōshiwake arimasen deshita" tte, ichido minna ni ayamattoita hō ga ī n ja nai?

> Ⓐ What should I do? Look at how shaken up everything has become.
>
> Ⓑ Maybe you should apologize to everyone and tell them you're sorry for having caused trouble?

★ **ayamaru** = apologize

133 顔に泥を塗る
かお どろ ぬ
Kao ni doro o nuru

Get mud on (your) face; make someone lose face

To cause someone to feel shame. To cause someone to lose face. Often preceded by「誰々の」.
だれだれ

Listen & Speak

1 Ⓐあなたのために社長がいろいろしてくれたんです。社長の
しゃちょう しゃちょう
顔に泥を塗るようなことはしないでくださいね。
かお どろ ぬ

Aanata no tame ni shachō ga iroiro shite kureta n desu. Shachō no kao ni doro o nuru yō na koto wa shinaide kudasai ne.

Ⓑはい。

Hai.

Ⓐ The president did a lot of things for your sake. Please don't do anything to make him lose face.
Ⓑ Okay.

★ *iroiro* = variously, in many ways

2 Ⓐじゃ、信じてるからね。
しん

Ja, shinjiteru kara ne.

Ⓑはい。先生のお顔に泥を塗るようなことはしません。
せんせい かお どろ ぬ

Hai. Sensē no o-kao ni doro o nuru yō na koto wa shimasen.

Ⓐ Okay, I'll believe you.
Ⓑ All right. I won't make you lose face, sensei.

★ *shinjiru* = believe

134 虫がいい

Selfish

Mushi ga ī

To brazenly say things for the benefit of only oneself. Often used to say something that benefits oneself while also being reflective and apologetic.

Listen & Speak

1 ご迷惑をおかけしておいて、こんなことを言うのは<u>虫がいい</u>のですが、支払いは月末まで待っていただけないでしょうか。

Go-mēwaku o o-kake shite oite, konna koto o yū no wa mushi ga ī no desu ga, shiharai wa getsumatsu made matte itadakenai de shō ka.

I know it is selfish of me to say this as it will cause you trouble, but could you wait until the end of the month for payment?

★ *shiharai* = payment
★ *getsumatsu* = end of month

2 Ⓐ 自分が悪いのはわかってるけど、給料は変わらないよね？

Jibun ga warui no wa wakatteru kedo, kyuryō wa kawaranai yo ne?

Ⓑ それはどうかな。ちょっと<u>虫がよすぎる</u>んじゃないかな。

Sore wa dō ka na. Chotto mushi ga yosugiru n ja nai ka na.

Ⓐ I know it's my fault, but my pay won't change, will it?

Ⓑ I don't know. Aren't you being a little too selfish?

★ *kyūryō* = salary, pay

飛ばす to fly, to let fly Useful One-word Expressions in Japanese 36

1. To go straight on without stopping   2. To make a vehicle go fast

Ex.1) 2、3ページ飛ばして読む／順番を飛ばされる
To skip one or two pages / to miss one's turn

Ex.2) タクシーを飛ばして来た。／時速120キロで飛ばした。
I made the taxi go fast. / I drove fast, at 120 kilometres an hour.

135 一からやり直す
いち　　　　　　　なお

Ichi kara yarinaosu

Start over from the beginning

To go back to the beginning and start again. To wipe clean.

1 Ⓐいろいろご心配おかけしましたが、引っ越して、一からや
しんぱい　　　　　　　　　　　　　　ひ　こ　　　　いち
り直してみます。
なお

*Iroiro go-shinpai o-kake shimashita ga, hikkoshite, ichi kara
yarinaoshite mimasu.*

Ⓑうん、それがいいよ。

Un, sore ga ī yo.

Ⓐ I know I've made you worry, but I'm
going to move and start over from the
beginning.

Ⓑ Yes, that would be best.

★ **go-shinpai o o-kake suru**
= honorific expression of
"*shinpai o kakeru*"

2 Ⓐあなたとはもう付き合わないことにしたの。
つ　あ

Anata towa mō tsukiawanai koto ni shita no.

Ⓑそんなこと言わないで。もう一度一からやり直そうよ。
い　　　　　　　　いち　ど　いち　　　　　なお

Sonna koto iwanaide. Mō ichido ichi kara yarinaosō yo.

Ⓐ I've decided not to see you any more.

Ⓑ Don't say that. Let's start over from
the beginning.

★ **tsukiau** = go out with, go
steady with

136 三日坊主
みっ か ぼう ず
Mikka bōzu

Fast quitter

To become easily bored and not continue something for a long time, or someone with such tendencies.

Listen & Speak

1 ❹私はだめ。ダイエットをしても、いつも三日坊主。
わたし　　　　　　　　　　　　　　　　　　　　みっ か ぼう ず
　　Watashi wa dame. Daietto o shite mo, itsumo mikka bōzu.

❸私も。続けるのって、大変だよね。
わたし　　つづ　　　　　　たいへん
　　Watashi mo. Tsuzukeru notte, taihen da yo ne.

❹ I'm hopeless. I try to diet, but I'm a fast quitter.
❸ Me too. It's so hard to keep going.

★ *tsuzukeru* = continue, keep on

2 ❹水泳教室はもうやめる。
すいえいきょうしつ
　　Suiē-kyōshitsu wa mō yameru.

❸えっ、また？この間、柔道やめたばかりじゃない。何でも
　　　　　　　　あいだ　じゅうどう　　　　　　　　　　　なん
三日坊主なんだから。
みっ か ぼう ず
　　Ett, mata? Konoaida, Jūdō yameta bakari ja nai. Nandemo mikka bōzu na n da kara.

❹ I'm quitting my swimming classes.
❸ What, again? You just quit judo the other day too. You're a fast quitter when it comes to anything.

★ *suiē* = swimming

137

やせ我慢をする
Yase-gaman o suru

Pretend to endure

To endure something unnecessarily and pretend one is calm.

Listen & Speak

1 Ⓐ寒そうだからコート貸したんだけど、着ないんだよ。

Samusō da kara kōto kashita n da kedo, kinai n da yo.

Ⓑ彼はいつも、そうやって<u>やせ我慢する</u>んですよ。

Kare wa itsumo, sō yatte yase-gaman suru n desu yo.

Ⓐ I let him borrow my coat because he seemed cold, but he won't wear it.

Ⓑ He always pretends to endure things like that.

★ **kōto** = coat

2 Ⓐ一人で大変なんだから、<u>やせ我慢</u>しないで手伝ってもらえば？

Hitori de taihen na n da kara, yase-gaman shinaide tesudatte moraeba?

Ⓑ別に<u>やせ我慢</u>なんてしてないよ。

Betsuni yase-gaman nante shite nai yo.

Ⓐ It's tough to do it alone, so instead of pretending you can manage, why don't you let someone help you?

Ⓑ I'm not pretending.

★ **betsu ni ~ nai** = not ~ in particular

線 line
せん

Direction or level

Ex) このサンプルはいい線行っている。／

「A案でいい？」「うん、その線で行こう」

This sample is just what we want. / "So Plan A's OK?" "Yes, let's go along those lines."

138 歯を食いしばる
Ha o kuishibaru

Grit one's teeth

To earnestly endure pain or difficulty. From the image of biting down hard and clenching one's teeth. Often followed by「我慢する」.

1 Ⓐそんなに<u>歯、食いしばって</u>ずっと我慢しなくてもいいんじゃない？　もっといい会社があるよ。

Sonnani ha, kuishibatte zutto gaman shinakute mo ī n ja nai? Motto ī kaisha ga aru yo.

Ⓑうん……。そうだね。

Un.... Sō da ne.

Ⓐ You don't have to grit your teeth and constantly endure things, do you? There are better companies.
Ⓑ Yeah… You're right.

★ **gaman suru** = put up with

2 Ⓐこのチーム強くなりましたね。

Kono chīmu tsuyoku narimashita ne.

Ⓑええ、みんな<u>歯を食いしばって</u>、厳しい練習に耐えてくれましたから。

Ē, minna ha o kuishibatte, kibishī renshū ni taete kuremashita kara.

Ⓐ This team has gotten stronger, hasn't it?
Ⓑ Yes, everyone grit their teeth and endured through severe practice.

★ **kibishī** = hard, harsh

157

139 お預け
あず
Oazuke

Postpone

To hold off on the realization or implementation of something due to some circumstance. Often followed by 「～を食う」.

* This term is sometimes used as a command to a dog to not eat food placed in front of it until permission is given.

Listen & Speak

1 Ⓐ 結婚式、どうだった？
けっこんしき
Kekkonsiki, dō datta?

Ⓑ うちの社長のスピーチがすごく長くて、ごちそうを前に
しゃちょう　　　　　　　　　　　　　　　　　　　　　　なが　　　　　　　　　　　まえ
ずっと<u>お預け</u>を食ったよ。
　　　　あず　　く
Uchi no shachō no supīchi ga sugoku nagakute, gochisō o mae ni zutto oazuke o kutta yo.

- -

Ⓐ How was the wedding ceremony?

Ⓑ Our president gave a really long speech, so the meal was postponed for the longest time.

★ *gochisō* = feast, banquet

2 Ⓐ 次の土日も仕事？
つぎ　どにち　しごと
Tsugi no donichi mo shigoto?

Ⓑ そう。ゴルフは当分<u>お預け</u>だよ。
　　　　　　　　とうぶん　あず
Sō. Gorufu wa tōbun oazuke da yo.

- -

Ⓐ Do you have work next weekend too?

Ⓑ Yes. Golf will have to be postponed for a while.

★ *tōbun* = for the time being

140 自腹を切る
じ　ばら　き
Jibara o kiru

Cover it yourself

To be responsible for a cost that one does not necessarily have to take on. 「自腹」 is an expression used to symbolize one's own money.
じばら

1 **Ⓐ** タクシー代、出るんですか。
だい　で
Takushī-dai, deru n desu ka?

Ⓑ うちの会社はケチだから、自腹切ることになるな。
かいしゃ　　　　　　　　　　じ　ばら　き
Uchi no kaisha wa kechi da kara, jibara kiru koto ni naru na.

Ⓐ Do you get reimbursed for taxi rides?
Ⓑ My company is stingy, so we have to cover it ourselves.

★ ***kechi (na)*** = stingy

2 **Ⓐ** この本は、先生が自腹を切って生徒全員に買ってくれたん
ほん　　　せんせい　じ　ばら　き　せいと　ぜんいん　か
だよ。
Kono hon wa, sensē ga jibara o kitte sēto zen'in ni katte kureta n da yo.

Ⓑ へー、いい先生だね。
せんせい
Hē, ī sensē da ne.

Ⓐ Our teacher bought copies of this book for all her students and covered it herself.
Ⓑ Wow, what a good teacher.

★ ***zen'in*** = all the members, all of ~

昼 noon
ひる

Useful One-word Expressions in Japanese 38

Lunch. Lunch is often referred to as "hiru"

Ex.) そろそろお昼にしましょう。／昼はいつも弁当です。／昼は何がいい？
ひる　　　　　　　　　　　　ひる　　　　べんとう　　　　ひる　なに
Let's have lunch soon. / I always have a packed lunch. / What do you want for lunch?

141 # 危ない橋を渡る

Cross a dangerous bridge

あぶ　はし　わた
Abunai hashi o wataru

To do something despite recognizing that it is dangerous. Sometimes used to refer to consciously breaking the law.

1 **Ⓐ**そこ、すごく危ない地域じゃない！　だめだよ。
　　あぶ　　ちいき

Soko, sugoku abunai chiiki ja nai! Dame da yo.

Ⓑうん。でも、<u>危ない橋を渡らない</u>と、撮れない写真もある
　　　　　　あぶ　はし　わた　　　　と　　　　しゃしん
から。

Un. Demo, abunai hashi o wataranai to torenai shashin mo aru kara.

> **Ⓐ** That's an incredibly dangerous area! You shouldn't.
> **Ⓑ** Yes, but there are some pictures you can't take unless you cross a dangerous bridge first.

★ **chiiki** = area

2 **Ⓐ**そんなに<u>危ない橋を渡らなくても</u>いいよ。失敗したら大変
　　　　　　あぶ　はし　わた　　　　　　　　しっぱい　　　　たいへん
だよ。

Sonnani abunai hashi o wataranakutemo ī yo. Shippai shitara taihen da yo.

Ⓑわかったよ。

Wakatta yo.

> **Ⓐ** You don't need to cross such a dangerous bridge. It'll be difficult if you fail.
> **Ⓑ** Okay, I understand.

★ **shippai suru** = fail

142 涙をのむ
なみだ
Namida o nomu

Choke back tears

To bear frustration. To hold back a desire to cry.

Listen & Speak

1 Ⓐ また決勝で負けて、涙をのんだよ。
けっしょう　ま　　　　なみだ
Mata kesshō de makete, naimda o nonda yo.

Ⓑ そうだったんだ。残念だったね。
ざんねん
Sō datta n da. Zannen datta ne.

Ⓐ We lost in the finals again, and I had to choke back tears.

Ⓑ Is that what happened? That's too bad.

★ **kesshō** = final game

2 Ⓐ パリに旅行するんでしょ？
りょこう
Pari ni ryokō suru n desho?

Ⓑ それが行けなくなったんです。仕事が忙しくて、涙をのん
い　　　　　　　　　　　　　　しごと　いそが　　　　　なみだ
であきらめたんです。

Sore ga ikenakunatta n desu. Shigoto ga isogashikute, namida o nonde akirameta n desu.

Ⓐ You're going to vacation in Paris, right?

Ⓑ We can't go after all. I'm so busy with work, so I had to choke back my tears and give up on it.

★ **akirameru** = give up

向こう beyond,
む　　other side

Useful One-word Expressions in Japanese 36

Another person, another person's company or home etc.

Ex.) 向こうに連絡する／向こうからの返事／向こうの担当者／向こうの親
む　　　　れんらく　　　む　　　　　　へんじ　　む　　　たんとうしゃ　　む　　　おや
To contact somebody (in another company) / a reply from the other person (or company) / the person responsible in another company/ another person's parents

143 砂をかむ
すな
Suna o kamu

Suffer through it

Something pointless, uninteresting, and dull. A situation that one is forced to reluctantly endure. Often followed by「〜な思い」.
おも

1 Ⓐ新しい仕事、どう？
あたら　しごと

Atarashī shigoto, dō?

Ⓑパソコン相手に毎日、<u>砂をかむ</u>ような思いだよ。
あいて　まいにち　すな　おも

Pasokon aite ni mainichi, suna o kamu yō na omoi da yo.

Ⓐ How's the new job?

Ⓑ I have to suffer through dealing with a computer every day.

★ *aite* = opponent, the other party

---

2 Ⓐ彼、新しい監督になってから、試合に全然出してもらえな
かれ　あたら　かんとく　しあい　ぜんぜん　だ
いね。

Kare, atarashī kantoku ni natte kara, shiai ni zenzen dashite moraenai ne.

Ⓑうん。<u>砂をかむ</u>ような思いで練習してるんじゃない？
すな　おも　れんしゅう

Un. Suna o kamu yō na omoi de renshū shiteru n ja nai?

Ⓐ He hasn't been able to play in matches at all since the new coach started.

Ⓑ Yes. He's probably having to suffer through it and just practice.

★ *kantoku* = head coach

---

144 息が詰まる
Iki ga tsumaru
(いき つ)

Feel like you're choking

To be forced into an oppressive, tense situation. A metaphor for being unable to breathe.

1 Ⓐ もう耐えられない、あの職場。誰も口きかないし、息が詰まりそう。
た しょくば だれ くち いき つ

Mō taerarenai, ano shokuba. Dare mo kuchi kikanai shi, iki ga tsumarisō.

Ⓑ じゃ、やめたら？

Ja, yametara?

Ⓐ I can't stand that workplace any more. No one listens to me, and it feels like I'm choking.

Ⓑ Then why don't you quit?

★ ***taeru*** = endure, withstand

2 Ⓐ あの人、ほんと、しゃべらないよね。
ひと

Ano hito, honto, shaberanai yo ne.

Ⓑ うん。一緒にいると息が詰まるよね。
いっしょ いき つ

Un. Issho ni iru to iki ga tsumaru yo ne.

Ⓐ He really doesn't talk, does he?

Ⓑ You're right. It feels like you're choking when you're with him.

★ ***issho ni iru*** = be (together) with

Ⓢ Dazed, unfocused, unenthusiastic

Ⓣ Having a problem, undesired situations or results, tight situations

Ⓤ To be embarrassed, to be reflective

Ⓥ To endure, to withstand difficulty, to make a sacrifice, to take a risk

Ⓦ To be extremely surprised, to feel fear

Ⓧ Suffering a mistake, being betrayed, something going wrong

Ⓨ Doing well and poorly, conditions going well and poorly

Ⓩ Other

INDEX

CD 73

145 ゾッとする
Zotto suru

Shudder

To feel surprised or in fear in a way that causes one's nerves to be rubbed the wrong way.

Listen & Speak

1 ❶ この前の電車の事故、怖かったですね。

Konomae no densha no jiko, kowakatta desu ne.

❷ はい、今でも思い出すとゾッとします。

Hai, ima demo omoidasu to zotto shimasu.

---

❶ The train accident the other day was scary, wasn't it?

❷ Yes, I still shudder when I think about it.

★ **kowai** = be scared

---

2 ❶ 昼間、こんな近くで事件が起こるなんて、ゾッとする。

Hiruma, konna chikaku de jiken ga okoru nante, zotto suru.

❷ うん。早く引っ越したいね。

Un. Hayaku hikkoshitai ne.

---

❶ It makes me shudder to think that an incident could happen in the middle of the day so close to here.

❷ Yes. I want to move quickly, don't you?

★ **jiken** = a matter of some trouble or crime

電気 electricity

Useful One-word Expressions in Japanese 40

1. An electric light   2. Electricity   3. Electrical goods

Ex.1) 電気をつける／電気が切れた。
To switch on the light / the lights have gone out.

Ex.3) 電気店
Electrical appliances shop

Ex.2) 電気料金／電気を無駄にしないでください。
Electricity bill/ Please don't waste electricity.

146 鳥肌が立つ
とりはだ た
Torihada ga tatsu

Get goosebumps

To feel fear, as in the sensation of fear causing one's skin to contract and feel like the skin of a bird. In recent times, the term is also often used in a positive way to say that one was emotionally moved.

Listen & Speak

1 Ⓐ そんな恐ろしい話、聞くだけで鳥肌が立つよ。
おそ はなし き とりはだ た
Sonna osoroshī hanashi, kiku dake de torihada ga tatsu yo.

Ⓑ そうだよね。
Sō da yo ne.

Ⓐ Just hearing something that scary gives you goosebumps.

Ⓑ It really does.

★ ***osoroshī*** = horrible, dreadful

2 Ⓐ 〈テレビの番組〉
ばんぐみ
ねえ、見て。これ、残酷だね。
み ざんこく
〈*Terebi no bangumi*〉
Nē, mite. Kore, zankoku da ne.

Ⓑ いいよ、もう。なんか鳥肌立ってきた。
とりはだ た
Ī yo, mō. Nanka torihada tatte kita.

Ⓐ 〈A TV program〉
Hey, look at this. Isn't it so cruel?

Ⓑ Oh, stop it. It's giving me goosebumps.

★ ***zankoku (na)*** = cruel

S Dazed, unfocused, unenthusiastic

T Having a problem, undesired situation or results, tight situations

U To be embarrassed, to be reflective

V To endure, withstand, difficulty, to make a sacrifice, to take a risk

W To be extremely surprised, to feel fear

X Suffering a mishap, being betrayed, something going wrong

Y Doing well and poorly, conditions going well and poorly

Z Other

INDEX

CD
74

147

血の気が引く
ち　　け　　　ひ
Chi no ke ga hiku

Turn pale

To become pale from fear.

Listen & Speak

1 Ⓐけさ運転してたら、小さい子が飛び出してきて、血の気が
うんてん　　　　　　　ちい　こ　　と　だ　　　　　　　ち　け
引いたよ。
ひ

Kesa unten shitetara, chīsai ko ga tobidashite kite, chi no ke ga hīta yo.

Ⓑ怖い。子供は危ないね。
こわ　　こども　　あぶ

Kowai. Kodomo wa abunai ne.

- - - - - - - - - -

Ⓐ A small child jumped out from nowhere when I was driving this morning, and it made me turn pale.

Ⓑ That's scary. A child? How dangerous.

★ **unten suru** = drive

2 Ⓐ誰？　こんな夜中に電話なんて。
だれ　　　　　よなか　でんわ

Dare? Konna yonaka ni denwa nante.

Ⓑほんと。何か悪い知らせかと、一瞬、血の気が引くよね。
なに　わる　し　　　　　いっしゅん　ち　け　ひ

Honto. Nanika warui shirase ka to, isshun, chi no ke ga hiku yo ne.

- - - - - - - - - -

Ⓐ Who would call like this in the middle of the night?

Ⓑ Really. It would make you turn pale for a moment with the thought that it's bad news.

★ **yonaka** = midnight

166

S Dazed, unfocused, unenthusiastic

T Having a problem, undesired situations or results, tight situations

U To be embarrassed, to be reflective

V To endure, to withstand difficulty, to make a sacrifice, to take a risk

W To be extremely surprised, to feel fear

X Suffering a mishap, being betrayed, something going wrong

Y Going well and poorly, conditions going well and poorly

Z Other

INDEX

148 # 寝耳に水
ね みみ みず
Nemimi ni mizu

Bolt from the blue

To be shocked to learn something unexpected. From the idea of being shocked by hearing the sound of water while sleeping.

1 **Ⓐ**来週からシンガポール支店に行ってくれって。<u>寝耳に水</u>だ
らいしゅう してん い ね みみ みず
よ。

Raishū kara Shingapōru-shiten ni itte kure tte. Nemimi ni mizu da yo.

Ⓑ大変なことになったね。
たいへん

Taihen na koto ni natta ne.

Ⓐ I was told to go to the Singapore branch starting next week. It was a bolt from the blue.

Ⓑ Sounds like things have gotten really tough.

★ *shiten* = branch

2 **Ⓐ**彼、独身主義だったんじゃなかったっけ？
かれ どくしんしゅ ぎ

Kare, dokushin-shugi datta n ja nakatta kke?

Ⓑそうなんだよ、だから、結婚したって話は本当に<u>寝耳に水</u>
けっこん はなし ほんとう ね みみ みず
だったんだよ。

Sō nan da yo. Dakara, kekkon shitatte hanashi wa hontō ni nemimi ni mizu na n da yo.

Ⓐ Didn't he swear he'd stay single?

Ⓑ Yes, so it was a bolt from the blue when I heard he got married.

★ *shugi* = one's principles

149 踏んだり蹴ったり Fundari kettari — One thing after another

To have awful things happen in succession.

Listen & Speak

1 Ⓐ最近の彼は<u>踏んだり蹴ったり</u>ですね。奥さんと離婚するし、けがをして入院するし。

Saikin no kare wa fundari kettari desu ne. Okusan to rikon suru shi, kega o shite nyūin suru shi.

Ⓐそうですね。

Sō desu ne.

Ⓐ It's been one thing after another for him lately. He got divorced from his wife, and then he was hospitalized with an injury.

Ⓑ You're right.

★ **rikon** = divorce

2 Ⓐどうしたの、そんな顔して。

Dōshita no, sonna kao shite.

Ⓑ今日は客に文句言われるし、財布を落とすし、もう<u>踏んだり蹴ったり</u>の日でした。

Kyō wa kyaku ni monku iwareru shi, saifu o otosu shi, mō fundari kettari no hi deshita.

Ⓐ What's the matter? Why do you look like that?

Ⓑ It's been one thing after another today. I had customers complain to me today, and I lost my wallet.

★ **monku o iu** = complain

150 # とばっちりを食う・とばっちりを受ける

Get mixed up in

Tobacchiri o kū / Tobacchiri o ukeru

「とばっちり」refers to splashed water. The phrase compares being close to water and getting splashed to being dragged into something.

Listen & Speak

1 Ⓐ 一人で騒いでいた友達のとばっちりを食って、僕も先生に怒られちゃったよ。

Hitori de sawaideita tomodachi no tobacchiri o kutte, boku mo sensē ni okorarechatta yo.

Ⓑ うそ。ついてないね。

Uso. Tsuitenai ne.

Ⓐ I got mixed up with my friend who was making a fuss on his own, and the teacher got mad at me too.

Ⓑ You poor thing. / No way. You're so unlucky.

★ *sawagu* = be noisy, make noise

2 Ⓐ 〈旅行中〉

ごめん、ごめん。田中がスマホなくしたって言うから、一緒に探してたんだ。

〈*Ryokō chū*〉

Gomen, gomen. Tanaka ga sumaho nakushita tte yū kara, issho ni sagashiteta n da.

Ⓑ 1時間も!?　とばっちり食ったね。

Ichi-jikan mo!? Tobacchiri kutta ne.

Ⓐ 〈During a trip〉

Sorry, sorry. Tanaka said he lost his smartphone, so I went with him to look for it.

Ⓑ For an hour?! You really got mixed up in that, didn't you?

★ *sawagu* = be noisy, make noise

169

151 痛い目にあう
いた　め
Itai me ni au

Have a terrible experience

To meet an awful fate.

1 Ⓐ お医者さんの言うこと、ちゃんと聞かないと、痛い目にあ
いしゃ　　い　　　　　　　　　　　き　　　　　　いた　め
うよ。

O-ishsa-san no yū koto, chanto kikanai to, itai me ni au yo.

Ⓑ 大丈夫だよ。
だいじょうぶ

Daijōbu da yo.

Ⓐ Something terrible will happen to you if you don't listen to what the doctor has to say.

Ⓑ I'll be fine.

★ *chanto* = properly, without fail

2 Ⓐ ここ1週間で急に円が上がりましたね。
しゅうかん　きゅう　えん　あ

Koko isshūkan de kyūni en ga agarimashita ne.

Ⓑ ええ。おかげで痛い目にあいましたよ。
いた　め

Ē. Okage de itai me ni aimashita yo.

Ⓐ The yen has suddenly risen over the past week, hasn't it?

Ⓑ Yes. I've had a terrible experience as a result.

★ *(sono) okage de* = thanks to it, owing to it

乗る to ride
の

Useful One-word Expressions in Japanese 41

1. To respond to someone's proposal   2. To go well with a movement or tune

Ex.1) 相談に乗る／誘いに乗る／話に乗る
そうだん　の　さそ　の　はなし　の
To get a consultation/to accept an invitation/to agree with someone

Ex.2) 音楽に乗る／調子に乗る
おんがく　の　ちょうし　の
Move to the beat of the music/ to get carried away

152

台無し
だ い な
Dainashi

Ruined

For something to be completely ruined. 「台」 here refers to a stand
だい
a Buddha statue is placed on, as without a stand the statue will be
damaged.

1 Ⓐ わあ、雨だ！ どうしよう。買ったばかりの着物が台無し
あめ か きもの だい な
になっちゃう。

*Wa, ameda! Dō shiyō. Katta bakari no kimono ga dainashi ni
nacchau.*

Ⓑ タクシー使えば？
つか

Takushī tsukaeba?

::::

Ⓐ Ah, it's raining! What should I do? The
kimono I just bought will be ruined.

Ⓑ Why don't you take a taxi?

★ *dō shiyō* = what can I do?

2 Ⓐ ごめんなさい。私のせいでみんなに迷惑かけちゃって。
わたし めいわく

Gomennasai. Watashi no sē de minna ni mēwaku kakechatte.

Ⓑ そんなに泣かないで。せっかくのお化粧が台無しだよ。
な けしょう だい な

Sonna ni nakanaide. Sekkaku no o-keshō ga dainashi da yo.

::::

Ⓐ I'm sorry. I ended up causing trouble for
everyone.

Ⓑ You don't need to cry so much. You'll
ruin the makeup you took time to put on.

★ *~ no sē de* = because of ~

★ *sekkaku no* = valuable,
rare, long-awaited

Listen & Speak

153 一杯食わされる

いっぱい く

Ippai kuwasareru

To be played; to be deceived

To be cleverly tricked into doing exactly what someone else wants.

 Listen & Speak

1 Ⓐ それ、偽物だよ。
にせもの

Sore, nisemono da yo.

Ⓑ しまった！ <u>一杯食わされ</u>ちゃった。お得ですよって言わ
いっぱい く　　　　　　　　　　とく　　　　　い
れて、つい。

Shimatta! Ippai kuwasarechatta. O-toku desu yo tte iwarete, tsui.

Ⓐ That's a fake.

Ⓑ Oh no! I was played. I was told it was a good deal, so I couldn't help myself.

★ *nisemono* = fake

2 Ⓐ 結局、お子さんに買ってあげたんですか。
けっきょく　　こ　　　か

Kekkyoku, o-ko-san ni katte ageta n desu ka?

Ⓑ ええ。クラスで自分だけ持ってないって言うから。でも、
じぶん　　も　　　　　　い
<u>一杯食わされた</u>みたいです。
いっぱい く

Ē. Kurasu de jibun dake mottenai tte yū kara. Demo, ippai kuwasareta mitai desu.

Ⓐ So you bought it for your child after all?

Ⓑ Yes, because she said she was the only one in her class that didn't have one. But it looks like she tricked me.

★ *kekkyoku* = at last, in the end

154 飼い犬に手をかまれる
か いぬ て

Kaiinu ni te o kamareru　　　　　Stabbed in the back

To be betrayed or harmed by someone one regularly takes care of.
A metaphor for being hurt when a pet dog bites its owner's hand.

Listen & Speak

1 Ⓐあの社長さん、長年勤めていた社員がライバル会社に移っ
しゃちょう ながねんつと しゃいん がいしゃ うつ
て怒ってたよ。
おこ

Ano shachō-san, naganen tsutometeita shain ga raibaru-gaisha ni utsutte okotteta yo.

Ⓑ<u>飼い犬に手をかまれた</u>ような気分だろうね。
か いぬ て きぶん

Kaiinu ni te o kamareta yō na kibun darō ne.

Ⓐ That company president was mad when an employee who had worked for him for many years went to a rival company.

Ⓑ He must feel like he was stabbed in the back.

★ *raibaru* = rival
★ *utsuru* = move

2 Ⓐ結構かわいがって面倒みてきた後輩なのに、会議で私の企
けっこう めんどう こうはい かいぎ わたし き
画に反対したんですよ。
かく はんたい

Kekkō kawaigatte mendō mitekita kōhai na noni, kaigi de watashi no kikaku ni hantai shita n desu yo.

Ⓑそうですか。<u>飼い犬に手をかまれた</u>ような感じですね。
か いぬ て かん

Sō desu ka. Kaiinu ni te o kamareta yō na kanji desu ne.

Ⓐ That was a junior I really took under my wing and looked after, yet he opposed my plan at the meeting.

Ⓑ Is that so. It must feel like you were stabbed in the back.

★ *kawaigaru* = treat with affection
★ *hantai suru* = oppose, disagree with

Ⓢ Dazed, unfocused, unenthusiastic

Ⓣ Having a problem, undesired situations or results, tight situations

Ⓤ To be embarrassed, to be reflective

Ⓥ To endure, to withstand difficulty, to make a sacrifice, to take a risk

Ⓦ To be extremely surprised, to feel fear

Ⓧ Suffering a mishap, being betrayed, something going wrong

Ⓨ Doing well and poorly, conditions going well and poorly

Ⓩ Other

INDEX

155 右肩上がり
みぎかたあ
Migikata-agari

Upward growth

A situation that becomes better the longer it goes on. A metaphor comparing a situation to a graph that rises as it stretches to the right. Often used in reference to numbers, such as regarding an economic situation.

Listen & Speak

1 **Ⓐ** この前出た新商品の売り上げはどうですか。
まえで しんしょうひん う あ

Kono mae deta shin-shōhin no uriage wa dō desu ka?

Ⓑ おかげさまで、<u>右肩上がり</u>で伸びてます。
みぎかたあ の

Okagesama de, migikata-agari de nobite masu.

Ⓐ How are the sales of the new product that was released the other day?

Ⓑ It's seeing upward growth, thanks to you.

★ ***okage sama de (=okage de)*** = thankfully, fortunately

2 **Ⓐ** 最近、売り上げ成績がずっと<u>右肩上がり</u>じゃない？
さいきん う あ せいせき みぎかたあ

Saikin, uriage-sēseki ga zutto migikata-agari ja nai?

Ⓑ ありがとうございます。

Arigatō gozaimasu.

Ⓐ Haven't sales results been seeing nothing but upward growth lately?

Ⓑ Thank you very much.

★ ***sēseki*** = performance, result

つぶす to crush　　**Useful One-word Expressions in Japanese 42**

To spend one's free time doing something

Ex.) 出発まで時間をつぶした。／一人で時間をつぶすのは大変だ。
しゅっぱつ じかん ひとり じかん たいへん
I killed time until my departure. / It's hard to kill time when you're alone.

156

うなぎ上り
のぼ

Unagi-nobori

Skyrocketing up

A sudden rise in evaluation or price due to some cause. Often used in reference to price, evaluation, or temperature. Eels move straight up, even in rapid streams. When one tries to grab an eel, they also attempt to escape straight upward. This expression comes from this disposition that eels have.

Listen & Speak

1 Ⓐ給料は上がらないのに、消費税が上がって物価も<u>うなぎ上り</u>。苦しいよ。
きゅうりょう　あ　　　　　しょうひぜい　あ　　　　ぶっか　　　　　　　　のぼ　　　くる

Kyūryō wa agaranai no ni, shōhizē ga agatte bukka mo unagi-nobori. Kurushī yo.

Ⓑ ほんとにそうだよね。

Honto ni sō da yo ne.

Ⓐ My salary isn't going up, but the sales tax is skyrocketing. It's difficult.

Ⓑ It really is.

★ **bukka** = prices of commodities

2 Ⓐ彼女が出ている映画、今、すごくヒットしてるね。
かのじょ　で　　　　　えいが　いま

Kanojo ga deteiru ēga, ima, sugoku hitto shiteru ne.

Ⓑ うん。彼女の人気も<u>うなぎ上り</u>なんだって。
かのじょ　にんき　　　　　　　　のぼ

Un. Kanojo no ninki mo unagi-nobori na n da tte.

Ⓐ The movie she's in is a huge hit, isn't it?

Ⓑ Yes. They say her popularity has been skyrocketing.

★ **ninki** = popularity

Ⓢ Dazed, unfocused, unenthusiastic

Ⓣ Having a problem, undesired situations or results, tight situations

Ⓤ To be embarrassed, to be reflective

Ⓥ To endure, to withstand difficulty, to make a sacrifice, to take a risk

Ⓦ To be extremely surprised, to feel fear

Ⓧ Suffering a mishap, being bothered, something going wrong

Ⓨ Doing well and poorly, conditions going well and poorly

Ⓩ Other

INDEX

157

頭打ち
あたま　う
Atama-uchi

Hit a peak

To reach a limit and to be unable to rise any higher. A metaphor for a situation where a highest possible level has been reached. Often used when indicating market prices or amounts.

Listen & Speak

1 Ⓐ 海外からの観光客が減ってるんだってね。
かいがい　　　　かんこうきゃく　へ

Kaigai kara no kankō-kyaku ga hetteru n da tte ne.

Ⓑ そうなんですよ、円高の影響で頭打ちなんです。
えんだか　えいきょう　あたまう

Sō nan desu yo, en-daka no ēkyō de atama-uchi nan desu.

Ⓐ They say the number of tourists from abroad is shrinking.

Ⓑ Yes, the effects of the strong yen have caused the number to hit a peak.

★ **ēkyō** = influence

2 Ⓐ 車の輸出量、頭打ちですね。
くるま　ゆしゅつりょう　あたまう

Kuruma no yushutsu-ryō, atama-uchi desu ne.

Ⓑ はい。他のアジアの国の車に押されてます。
ほか　　　　　くに　くるま　お

Hai, hoka no Ajia no kuni no kuruma ni osarete masu.

Ⓐ The number of exported cars has hit a peak, hasn't it?

Ⓑ Yes. We're being pressured by cars from other Asian countries.

★ **yushutsu (suru)** = export

捕まえる to catch
つか

Useful One-word Expressions in Japanese 43

To call to a person to stop

Ex.) 部長が帰る前に捕まえよう。／タクシーを捕まえる
ぶちょう　かえ　まえ　つか　　　　　　　　　　つか
Let's catch the manager before she goes home. / To catch a taxi

158 # 足踏み
あし　ぶ
Ashibumi

Standstill

To not move forward and stay stagnant. A metaphor comparing a situation to standing still in one place. Often followed by「〜状態」.
じょうたい
Used not just for numbers but also about human relationships and life.

Listen & Speak

1 Ⓐ マンションの売れ行き、いいみたいね。
　　　　　　　　う　ゆ
　　Manshon no ureyuki, ī mitai ne.

　Ⓑ いえ、そうでもないです。足踏み状態です、今は。
　　　　　　　　　　　　　　　あし　ぶ　じょうたい　　　いま
　　Ie, sō demo nai desu. Ashibumi-jōtai desu, ima wa.

Ⓐ Condominium sales seem to be strong.
Ⓑ No, they aren't. They're currently at a standstill.

★ *manshon* = apartment
★ *ureyuki* = sales

2 Ⓐ 例の契約、ずっと足踏み状態らしいよ。
　　　れい　けいやく　　　　あし　ぶ　じょうたい
　　Rē no kēyaku, zutto ashibumi-jōtai rashī yo.

　Ⓑ そうなんだ。うまく行くといいんだけどね。
　　　　　　　　　　　　い
　　Sō na n da. Umaku iku to ī n da kedo ne.

Ⓐ Seems like the contract has been at a standstill for a while.
Ⓑ I see. I do hope it goes well.

★ *kēyaku* = contract

拾う *to pick up*
ひろ

Useful One-word Expressions in Japanese 44

1. To find something you need　　2. To catch a taxi

Ex.1) キーワードを拾う／間違いを拾う
　　　　　　　　ひろ　　まちが　　ひろ
　　　To find the key word/ to spot the mistake

Ex.2) タクシーを拾う
　　　　　　　　ひろ
　　　To catch a taxi

S Dazed, unfocused, unenthusiastic

T Having a problem, undesired situations or results, tight situations

U To be embarrassed, to be reflective

V To endure, to withstand difficulty, to make a sacrifice, to take a risk

W To be extremely surprised, to feel fear

X Suffering a mishap, being betrayed, something going wrong

Y Doing well and poorly, conditions going well and poorly

Z Other

INDEX

159 追い風
お かぜ
Oikaze

Tailwind

A favorable situation. Often used in the form 「○○ (the reason or cause for a favorable situation) が追い風と (に) なる」.
お かぜ

1 Ⓐ オリンピックが追い風になって、柔道教室でも生徒が増え
お かぜ じゅうどうきょうしつ せいと ふ
ています。

Orinpikku ga oikaze ni natte, jūdō-kyōshitsu demo sēto ga fuete imasu.

Ⓑ そうですか。それはよかったですね。

Sō desu ka. Sore wa yokatta desu ne.

Ⓐ The Olympics have acted as a tailwind, and students in judo classrooms have been increasing.

Ⓑ Is that so? That's good to hear.

★ *fueru* = increase

2 Ⓐ 最近、この人の本が目立つね。
さいきん ひと ほん めだ
Saikin, kono hito no hon ga medatsu ne.

Ⓑ やはり直木賞受賞が追い風になってるんじゃない？
なお き しょうじゅしょう お かぜ
Yahari Naoki-shō jushō ga oikaze ni natteru n ja nai?

Ⓐ This person's books have stood out lately, wouldn't you say?

Ⓑ Her winning the Naoki Prize must be acting as a tailwind.

★ *jushō* = winning prize

160

逆風
ぎゃくふう
gyakufū

Headwind

An unfavorable situation or tendency. Often used in the form 「○○
（the reason or cause for an unfavorable situation）が逆風となる」.
ぎゃくふう

Listen
&
Speak

1 Ⓐ 今年は雪が降りすぎたのが逆風となって、スキー客が減っ
こ　とし　ゆき　ふ　　　　　　ぎゃくふう　　　　　　　　　　　きゃく　　へ
たみたい。

*Kotoshi wa yuki ga furisugi na no ga gyakufū to natte, sukī-kyaku
ga hetta mitai.*

Ⓑ へえ、そうなんだ。

Hē, sō na n da.

Ⓐ It seems that too much snowfall this year
has acted as a headwind, and the number
of skiers has gone down.

Ⓑ Oh, really?

★ **heru** = decrease

2 Ⓐ 円安が逆風となって、海外旅行に行く人が減ってるらしい
えんやす　　ぎゃくふう　　　　　　かいがいりょこう　い　ひと　　へ
よ。

*En-yasu ga gyakufū to natte, kaigai-ryokō ni iku hito ga hetteru
rashī yo.*

Ⓑ そりゃ、そうだろうね。

Sorya, sō darō ne.

Ⓐ It seems the weak yen has acted as a
headwind, and the number of people going
on trips abroad has decreased.

Ⓑ Well, that makes sense.

★ **en-yasu** = weak yen

Ⓢ Dazed, unfocused, unenthusiastic

Ⓣ Having a problem, undesired situations or results, tight situations

Ⓤ To be embarrassed, to be reflective

Ⓥ To endure a difficulty, to withstand, to make a sacrifice, to take a risk

Ⓦ To be extremely surprised, to feel fear

Ⓧ Suffering a mishap, being betrayed, something going wrong

Ⓨ Doing well and poorly, conditions going well and poorly

Ⓩ Other

INDEX

161 空回り
からまわ
Karamawari

Spinning one's wheels

A situation where no amount of effort brings about results. A metaphor comparing a situation to car wheels that spin uselessly instead of moving as they were meant to do.

Listen & Speak

1 Ⓐ ダンスがうまくなりたくて、夜遅くまで練習しているんだけど、なかなか上達しない。

Dansu ga umaku naritakute, yoru osoku made renshū shiteiru n da kedo, nakanaka jōtatsu shinai.

Ⓑ 空回りしてるんじゃない？ ちゃんと休んだほうがいいよ。

Karamawari shiteru n ja nai? Chanto yasunda hō ga ī yo.

Ⓐ I want to become better at dancing so I've been practicing until late in the night, but I don't seem to be getting much better.

Ⓑ Aren't you just spinning your wheels? It would be better for you get some proper rest.

★ *jōtatsu suru* = make progress in

2 Ⓐ どうだった？ 相手は許してくれた？

Dō datta? Aite wa yurushite kureta?

Ⓑ どうかなあ。丁寧に説明しようとしたら、言い訳が多くなっちゃって……。空回りしてたかも。

Dō ka nā. Tēnē ni setsumē shiyō to shitara, ī wake ga ōku nacchatte.... Karamawari shiteta kamo.

Ⓐ How was it? Did they forgive you?

Ⓑ I don't know. I tried to give a proper explanation, but I ended up giving a lot of excuses... I might have been spinning my wheels.

★ *yurusu* = forgive someone

162 痛しかゆし
いた
Itashi-kayushi

Choosing between two evils; mixed blessing

A situation where choosing either of two options will create difficulty in another way. A metaphor comparing a situation to scratching something leading to pain, while not scratching something causing it to itch.

1 Ⓐ値段を下げれば売れる数は増えるけど、利益も小さくなる
ね だん さ う かず ふ り えき ちい
し。痛しかゆしだね。
いた

Nedan o sagereba ureru kazu wa fueru kedo, rieki mo chīsaku naru shi. Itashi-kayushi da ne.

Ⓑなかなか難しいね。
むずか

Nakanaka muzukashī ne.

┈┈┈┈┈┈┈┈┈┈┈┈┈┈┈┈┈┈

Ⓐ We'll sell more if we lower the price, but we'll make less profit too. It's a choice between two evils.

Ⓑ Sounds pretty difficult.

★ *rieki* = profit

2 Ⓐアパート、学校のすぐそばなんだね。近くていいね。
がっこう ちか

Apāto, gakkō no sugu soba na n da ne. Chikakute ī ne.

Ⓑまあね。でも、友達がすぐ遊びに来るから、困ることもあ
ともだち あそ く こま
る。痛しかゆしだね。
いた

Mā ne. Demo, tomodachi ga sugu asobi ni kuru kara, komaru koto mo aru. Itashi-kayushi da ne.

┈┈┈┈┈┈┈┈┈┈┈┈┈┈┈┈┈┈

Ⓐ Your apartment is right next to school. It must be nice to be so close.

Ⓑ I guess. But it can also be troubling, because my friends are quick to come over to play. It's a mixed blessing.

★ *(~ no) sugu soba (ni)* = nearby, close by~

Listen & Speak

S Dazed, unfocused, unenthusiastic

T Having a problem, undesired situations or reality, tight situations

U To be embarrassed, to be reflective

V To endure, to withstand, to make a sacrifice, to take a risk

W To be extremely surprised, to feel fear

X Suffering & mishap, being betrayed, something going wrong

Y Doing well and poorly, conditions going well and poorly

Z Other

INDEX

163 ## ご機嫌斜め
き げん なな
Go-kigen naname

Crabby

To be in a poor mood. Used especially in reference to one's superiors, or those seen as important or in high positions. Because of this the honorific「ご」is used with「機嫌」.
き げん

1 Ⓐ部長、朝からご機嫌斜めですね。
ぶ ちょう あさ き げん なな
Buchō, asa kara go-kigen naname desu ne.

Ⓑそう、そう。あまりそばに寄らないほうがいいよ。
よ
Sō, sō. Amari soba ni yoranai hō ga ī yo.

Ⓐ The department chief seems to have been crabby since the morning.

Ⓑ Yes, that's right. I wouldn't get too close to him.

★ *soba ni yoru(=chikazuku)* = come near

2 Ⓐ〈会社の退社時間〉
かいしゃ たいしゃ じ かん
今日は早いですね。
きょう はや
〈*Kaisha no taisha jikan*〉
Kyō wa hayai desu ne.

Ⓑまあね。最近、帰りが遅いって、うちの奥さんがご機嫌斜
さいきん かえ おそ おく き げん なな
めで。
Mā ne. Saikin, kaeri ga osoi tte, uchi no okusan ga go-kigen naname de.

Ⓐ〈When leaving work〉
You're early today.

Ⓑ Well, I've been getting back late recently, and my wife has been crabby.

★ *uchi no okusan (=uchi no tsuma)* = my wife

164 へそを曲げる

Heso o mageru

Peevish

To be offended and act obstinately as a result. Often used as a noun expression in the form of「へそ曲_まがり」.

1 **Ⓐ** なんだか雰囲気悪いね。
ふん い き わる

Nandaka fun'iki warui ne.

Ⓑ そうなんです。先に部長に相談したことがバレて、課長が
さき ぶ ちょう そうだん か ちょう
へそ曲げてしまって。
ま

Sō na n desu. Sakini buchō ni sōdan shita koto ga barete, kachō ga heso magete shimatte.

Ⓐ There seems to be something bad in the air.

Ⓑ There is. The section chief just found out I had a talk with the department chief, and he's been acting peevishly.

★ *fun'iki* = atmosphere

2 **Ⓐ** もう、あなたのご飯作りませんから！
はんつく

Mō, anata no gohan tsukurimasen kara!

Ⓑ そんなにへそ曲げないでよ。
ま

Sonna ni heso magenaide yo.

Ⓐ Fine, I'm not making dinner for you anymore.

Ⓑ Don't act so peevishly.

★ *sonna ni* = so, so ~, too ~, so much, like that

165 首を縦に振る
くび たて ふ
Kubi o tate ni furu

Nod yes

To consent. A metaphor comparing one's actions to the affirmative expression of nodding one's head up and down.

1 Ⓐ この間の件、その後、どうでしょうか。
あいだ けん ご

Kono aida no ken, sono go, dō de shō ka.

Ⓑ 申し訳ありません、上司がなかなか首を縦に振ってくれな
もう わけ じょうし くび たて ふ
いんです。

Mōshiwake arimasen. Jōshi ga nakanaka kubi o tate ni futte kurenai n desu.

Ⓐ So, how did it go after all that?

Ⓑ I'm sorry, my boss just wouldn't give me the nod yes.

★ **kono aida (no)** = the other day, a little while ago, last

★ **ken** = matter

2 Ⓐ 何度も通って、説明して、やっと社長さんが首を縦に振っ
なんど かよ せつめい しゃちょう くび たて ふ
てくれました。

Nando mo kayotte, setsumē shite, yatto shachō-san ga kubi o tate ni futte kuremashita.

Ⓑ よかったですね。

Yokatta desu ne.

Ⓐ I went again and again to explain, and the president finally nodded yes.

Ⓑ That's great.

★ **setsumē suru** = explain

166

鬼のように
おに
Oni no yō ni

Like the devil

An expression used to strengthen the word it precedes, as if to say "a lot" or "extremely." A metaphor comparing something to the frightening and powerful presence of the devil. Used in casual speech.

Listen & Speak

1 Ⓐ 監督、怒ってた？
かんとく　おこ
Kantoku, okotteta?

Ⓑ 鬼のように怒ってたけど。どうしたの？
おに　　　　　おこ
Oni no yō ni okotteta kedo. Dō shita no?

Ⓐ Was the coach mad?
Ⓑ He was mad like the devil. What happened?

★ ***kantoku*** = director, head coach

2 Ⓐ 今、鬼のように忙しいから、返事はしばらく待ってください。
いま　おに　　　　　いそが　　　　　　へんじ　　　　　　　　ま
Ima, oni no yō ni isogashī kara, henji wa shibaraku matte kudasai.

Ⓑ わかりました。
Wakarimashita.

Ⓐ I'm as busy as the devil right now, so please wait for a bit on a response.
Ⓑ Understood.

★ ***shibaraku (no aida)*** = a (little) while, for the time being

167

耳を傾ける
みみ　　かたむ
Mimi o katamukeru

Give an ear

To listen passionately or attentively. A metaphor comparing a situation to the action of pointing one's ear toward someone else. Used not about oneself but when describing a situation where a superior is the subject.

1 Ⓐ 先生が兄の話に<u>耳を傾けて</u>くださいましたので、事情は理
せんせい　あに　はなし　　みみ　かたむ　　　　　　　　　　じじょう　り
解してくださったと思います。
かい　　　　　　　　　おも

Sensē ga ani no hanashi ni mimi o katamukete kudasaimashita node, jijō wa rikai shite kudasatta to omoimasu.

Ⓑ そうですか。

Sō desu ka.

Ⓐ Sensei gave an ear to what my older brother had to say, so I think she understands the circumstances.

Ⓑ Is that so?

★ *jijō* = situation, the state of things

2 Ⓐ 昨日の講演会はどうでしたか。
きのう　こうえんかい

Kinō no kōenkai wa dō deshita ka?

Ⓑ よかったですよ。参加者の方は皆、集中して話に<u>耳を傾け</u>
さんかしゃ　かた　みな　しゅうちゅう　　はなし　みみ　かたむ
てました。

Yokatta desu yo. Sankasha no kata wa mina, shūchū shite hanashi ni mimi o katamukete mashita.

Ⓐ How was yesterday's lecture?

Ⓑ It went well. The participants were all focused and gave an ear to what was being said.

★ *kōenkai* = lecture meeting
★ *shūchū suru* = concentrate

168 目を通す
<ruby>目<rt>め</rt></ruby>を<ruby>通<rt>とお</rt></ruby>す

Look over

Me o tōsu

To take a quick look through. Used in situation such as when asking a busy superior to read through something.

1 ❶はい、お<ruby>呼<rt>よ</rt></ruby>びでしょうか。

Hai, oyobideshō ka.

❷<ruby>悪<rt>わる</rt></ruby>いけど、これにすぐ<u>目を通して</u>、<ruby>間違<rt>まちが</rt></ruby>いがないかどうかチェックしてくれる？

Waruikedo, kore ni sugu me o tōshite, machigai ga nai ka dō ka, chekku shite kureru?

❶ Yes, did you call for me?
❷ I'm sorry, but could you look over this immediately and check to see if there are any mistakes?

★ *warui kedo….* = I'm sorry, but….

2 ❶お<ruby>忙<rt>いそが</rt></ruby>しいところ<ruby>申<rt>もう</rt></ruby>し<ruby>訳<rt>わけ</rt></ruby>ありませんが、ざっと<u>お<ruby>目<rt>め</rt></ruby>通し</u>いただけますでしょうか。

O-isogashī tokoro mōshiwake arimasen ga, zatto o-me-dōshi itadakemasu de shō ka.

❷わかりました。

Wakarimashita.

❶ I'm sorry to bother you when you're busy, but could you take a look over this?
❷ Okay.

★ *zatto* = roughly
★ *o-me-dōshi* = honorific expression of "*me o tōsu koto*"

187

CD
85

169

ドタキャン

Dotakyan

Last-second cancelation

To cancel at the last moment. Used as spoken language, and should be avoided in formal situations.

Listen & Speak

1 Ⓐ えっ、この人、またドタキャン？
Ett, kono hito, mata dotakyan?

Ⓑ そうなんだ。これで三度目。
Sō nan da. Kore de san-do-me.

Ⓐ What? He canceled at the last second again?

Ⓑ That's right. This makes it three times.

★ *~ do-me (~ kai-me)* = ~ th

2 Ⓐ 15日、ほんとに来られるの？
Jūgo-nich, honto ni korareru no?

Ⓑ 大丈夫だよ。ドタキャンなんかしないから。
Daijōbu da yo. Dotakyan nanka shinai kara.

Ⓐ Can you really come on the 15th?

Ⓑ Don't worry. I won't cancel at the last second.

★ *honto ni* = really

 手 hand
て

Useful One-word Expressions in Japanese 45

I. A method 2. Work, a working person 3. Time or trouble

Ex.1) 何かいい手はないですか。
なに　　　て
Isn't there a good way?

Ex.3) 手がかかる
て
To need a lot of looking after

Ex.2) 手を貸す／手が足りない／働き手
て　か　　て　た　　　　はたら　て
To lend a hand / not have enough workers / worker

170 **朝一・午後一**
あさ いち ご ご いち
Asaichi / Gogoichi

First thing in the morning / afternoon

「朝一」 refers to immediately after morning business begins, while
あさいち
「午後一」 refers to immediately after lunch break when afternoon
ご ご いち
business begins. A shortening of 「朝一番」 and 「午後一番」, as
                                あさいちばん   ご ご いちばん
four-syllable terms are easier to say.

Listen & Speak

1 Ⓐ じゃ、よろしくお願いします。
                        ねが
 Ja, yoroshiku onegai shimasu.

 Ⓑ わかりました、明日、朝一でご連絡します。
              あした あさいち れんらく
 Wakarimashita, ashita, asaichi de go-renraku shimasu.

 Ⓐ I'll be counting on you.
 Ⓑ All right. I will contact you first thing in the morning.

 ★ *renraku suru* = contact, get in touch with

2 Ⓐ すみません、急いでるので、午後一でお願いできますか。
              いそ ご ご いち ねが
 Sumimasen, isoideru node, gogo-ichi de onegai dekimasu ka?

 Ⓑ かしこまりました。
 Kashikomarimashita.

 Ⓐ Excuse me, I'm in a rush, so could I have it first thing in the afternoon?
 Ⓑ Understood.

 ★ *kashikomarimashita* = honorific expression of "*wakarimashita*"

Useful One-word Expressions in Japanese 46

足 foot, leg
あし

Means of transport, vehicle

Ex.) 田舎は足がなくて困る。／市民の足
     いなか あし   こま   しみん あし
 I have a hard time as there's no way to get around in the countryside./Public transport

CD
86

171

すし詰め

Packed like sardines

Sushizume

When people are objects are gathered in a single space that is so crowded there is no room between them. An expression comparing a situation to rice used in pressed sushi that is packed together in a box during the making process.

Listen & Speak

1 Ⓐ 東京で、すし詰めの満員電車、初めて体験しました。

とうきょう　　　　づ　　　　まんいんでんしゃ　　はじ　　　　たいけん

Tōkyō de, sushizume no man'in-densha, hajimete taiken shimashita.

Ⓑ そうでしたか。あれ、本当に大変ですよね。

ほんとう　　たいへん

Sō deshita ka. Are, hontō ni taihen desu yo ne.

> Ⓐ I experienced my first train packed like sardines in Tokyo.
>
> Ⓑ Really. Those are really tough, aren't they?

> ★ **taiken suru** = experience

2 Ⓐ 昨日の花火大会、人がすごかったみたいですね。

きのう　　はなびたいかい　　ひと

Kinō no hanabi-taikai, hito ga sugokatta mitai desu ne.

Ⓑ そうなんです。一番眺めのいい会場は、すし詰め状態でしたよ。

いちばんなが　　　　　かいじょう　　　　　　づ　じょうたい

Sō nan desu. Ichiban nagame no ī kaijō wa, sushizume jōtai deshita yo.

> Ⓐ It sounds like there were a lot of people at yesterday's fireworks display.
>
> Ⓑ There were. People were packed like sardines in the area with the best view.

> ★ **hito** = the number of people
> ★ **sugoi** = amazing

172 いもづる式

しき

Imozuru-shiki

One after another

For something to continue on and on. A comparison of a situation to pulling the vine of a sweet potato, causing many connected potatoes to come out of the ground.

1 Ⓐ犯人、捕まった？
はんにん　つか

Hannin, tsukamatta?

Ⓑうん。一人捕まったら、<u>いもづる式</u>に捕まったらしいよ。
ひとり つか　　　　　　　　　しき　つか

Un. Hitori tsukamattara, imozuru-shiki ni tsukamatta rashī yo.

Ⓐ Did they catch the culprits?

Ⓑ Yes. Once they caught one, they seem to have arrested the others one after another.

★ **hannin** = criminal

2 Ⓐすごい！　全部売れたの？
ぜん ぶ う

Sugoi! Zenbu ureta no?

Ⓑはい。まず、一人の奥さんが買ってくれて、それから、<u>い</u>
ひと り　おく　　　　か
<u>もづる式</u>に皆さんが買ってくれたんです。
しき　みな　　　　か

Hai. Mazu, hitori no okusan ga katte kurete, sorekara, imozuru-shiki ni minasan ga katte kureta n desu.

Ⓐ Wow! You sold them all?

Ⓑ Yes. Once one lady bought one, everyone else bought them one after another.

★ **okusan** = a way of saying "housewife" or "lady (especially middle age)"

173 しわ寄せ

Shiwayose

Bear a burden; take a toll

When something's negative effect influences other things as well. A comparison of a situation to trying to get rid of a wrinkle causing more wrinkles to appear elsewhere. Often used with 「〜が来る」 or 「〜が行く」.

1 Ⓐ 石油の価格が上がると、そのしわ寄せで、いろいろな物の値段が上がるんだよ。

Sekiyu no kakaku ga agaru to, sono shiwayose de, iroiro na mono no nedan ga agaru n da yo.

Ⓑ そうなんだ。

Sō na n da.

Ⓐ When the price of oil goes up, it also takes a toll on many other things, causing their prices to go up.

Ⓑ That's right.

★ **sekiyu** = petroleum

---

2 Ⓐ また、徹夜しちゃった。

Mata, tesuya shichatta.

Ⓑ よくないなあ。無理をしたら、どこかにしわ寄せが来るよ。

Yokunai nā. Muri o shitara, dokoka ni shiwayose ga kuru yo.

Ⓐ I pulled another all-nighter.

Ⓑ That's not good. Working yourself too hard is going to take a toll on you somehow.

★ **tetsuya suru** = sit up all night

174

二番煎じ
に ばん せん じ
Niban-senji

Rehash

For something to appear the same as it was before and to have no new charm. To repeat something, causing it to be uninteresting. From the act of extracting tea or medicinal plants twice, causing the effects to be weaker.

Listen & Speak

1

A 今、健康ブームだから、こういう企画はどうですか。
いま けんこう きかく
Ima, kenkō-būmu da kara, kōyū kikaku wa dō desu ka?

B それじゃ、ほかの会社の二番煎じになるだけじゃないか。
かいしゃ に ばんせん
Sore ja, hoka no kaisha no niban-senji ni naru dake ja naika.

A There's a health fad right now, so how about this plan?

B That would just be a rehash of what other companies do.

★ *kikaku* = plan, project

2

A この映画、どこかで見たことがあるような話だね。
えい が み はなし
Kono ēga, dokoka de mita koto ga aru yō na hanashi da ne.

B どうせ何かの二番煎じだよ。
なに に ばんせん
Dōse nanika no niban-senji da yo.

A I feel like I've seen this movie somewhere before.

B It's just a rehash of something else.

★ *dokoka de* = somewhere

人 person
ひと

 Useful One-word Expressions in Japanese 47

1. People 2. Other people 3. Human beings

Ex.1) ここはいつも人が多い。／若い人
ひと おお わか ひと
There are always lots of people here. /Young people

Ex.2) 人の悪口を言う／人に聞いたほうがいい。
ひと わるぐち い ひと き
To say unkind things about other people/ You should ask somebody.

Ex.3) 人が食べるもの／人の体
ひと た ひと からだ
Things human beings eat / the human body

Right side tab labels:
S Dazed, unfocused, unenthusiastic
T Having a problem, undesired situations or results, tight situations
U To be embarrassed, to be reflective
V To endure, difficulty, to make a sacrifice, to take a risk
W To be extremely surprised, to feel fear
X Suffering a mishap, being betrayed, something going wrong
Y Doing well and poorly, conditions going well and poorly
Z Other
INDEX

175 盲点
もうてん
Mōten

Blind spot

To carelessly overlook something. A spot in one's vision that one cannot see due to the way the eye is constructed. Often used in the forms「盲点がある」and「盲点を突く」.

Listen & Speak

1 Ⓐ ホームページを見たお客さんが、キャンセルの仕方がわからないって。

Hōmupēji o mita okyaku-san ga, kyanseru no shikata ga wakaranai tte.

Ⓑ そうか。それは<u>盲点</u>だったなあ。

Sō ka. Sore wa mōten datta nā.

Ⓐ Customers who look at our website say they can't figure out how to cancel.

Ⓑ Oh. That was a blind spot.

★ **~ no shikata** = how to do ~

2 Ⓐ あの人、頭いいよね。うまいことして儲けたんだ。

Ano hito, atama ī yo ne. Umai koto shite mōketa n da.

Ⓑ うん。法律の<u>盲点</u>を突いたんだね。

Un. Hōritsu no mōten o tsuita n da ne.

Ⓐ She's smart, isn't she? She made money in a clever way.

Ⓑ Yes. She used a blind spot in the law.

★ **mōkeru** = make money, make a profit

ところ a place
Useful One-word Expressions in Japanese

I. Part, point 2. Just at that moment

Ex.I) 悪いところを直す。／この白いところに書いてください。
To fix a faulty part. / Please write in the white space.

Ex.2) 今、駅に着いたところです。
I've just arrived at the station

176 落とし穴
Otoshiana

Trap; pitfall

A careless failure, error, or defect. From a type of trap that is a hole dug in the ground in order to capture animals.

Listen & Speak

1 **Ⓐ** ネットビジネスなら、始めるのに費用があまりかからないから始めやすいよね。

Netto-bijinesu nara, hajimeru no ni hiyō ga amari kakaranai kara hajimeyasui yo ne.

Ⓑ そうだけど、気をつけないと<u>落とし穴</u>もあると思うよ。

Sō da kedo, ki o tsukenai to otoshiana mo aru to omou yo.

Ⓐ It's easy to start an online business because the initial costs aren't very high.

Ⓑ Yes, but I think there can also be pitfalls if you're not careful.

★ *hiyō* = cost

2 **Ⓐ** カロリー制限ダイエットって、効果があるけど、<u>落とし穴</u>もあるよね。

Karorī-sēgen daietto tte, kōka ga aru kedo, otoshiana mo aru yo ne.

Ⓑ うん。カロリーばかり気にすると、栄養が偏るからね。

Un. Karorī bakari ki ni suru to, ēyō ga katayoru kara ne.

Ⓐ Calorie-restricting diets can have pitfalls, too. / Calorie-restricting diets are effective, but they have pitfalls, too.

Ⓑ Yes. If you're concerned only about calories, your nutrition can become unbalanced.

★ *ēyō* = nutrition
★ *katayoru* = be biased, be one-sided, lean towards ~

Z | Other

 CD 89

177 # 思うツボ
おも
Omou tsubo

As one wished; play into someone's hands

To acquire results that were exactly what one hoped for. A comparison of a situation to a gambler rolling dice into a cup and getting the exact result they hoped for. Used in the form 「○○の思うツボ」, with enemies or rivals that one would not want to get their way often used in ○○．To acquire results that were exactly what one hoped for. A comparison of a situation to a gambler rolling dice into a cup and getting the exact result they hoped for. Used in the form 「○○の思う ツボ」, with enemies or rivals that one would not want to get their way often used in ○○．

 Listen & Speak

1 Ⓐ ボールを持ったら、どんどん攻めよう。
も　　　　　　　　　　　　せ

Bōru o mottara, dondon semeyō.

Ⓑ それじゃ、向こうの<u>思うツボ</u>だよ。前回と違うやり方を考
む　　　　　おも　　　　　　　ぜんかい　ちが　　　かた　かんが
えないと。

Sore ja, mukō no omou tsubo da yo. Zenkai to chigau yarikata o kangaenai to.

Ⓐ Let's charge forward and attack once we get the ball.

Ⓑ That'd play right into their hands. We need to come up with something different compared to last time.

★ ***semeru*** = attack

2 Ⓐ これもついでに買っちゃう？
か

Kore mo tsuide ni kacchau?

Ⓑ いらないよ、そんなの。気をつけないと、店側の<u>思うツボ</u>だよ。
き　　　　　　　　みせがわ　おも

Iranai yo, sonna no. Ki o tsukenai to, mise-gawa no omou tsubo da yo.

Ⓐ Do you want to buy this too?

Ⓑ We don't need that. You need to be careful, or else you'll play right into the store's hands.

★ ***tsuide ni*** = in addition, in passing

196

178 ふるいにかける

Furui ni kakeru

Screen; separate the wheat from the chaff

To select the good things among many choices. From the act of using a sieve to separate coarse grains.

Listen & Speak

1 **Ⓐ**思った以上に応募者が多いね。
_{おも} _{い じょう} _{おう ぼ しゃ} _{おお}

Omotta ijō ni ōbo-sha ga ōi ne.

Ⓑそうですね。まず、書類で<u>ふるいにかけ</u>ましょうか。
_{しょるい}

Sō desu ne. Mazu, shorui de furui ni kakemashō ka.

Ⓐ We had more applicants than we expected.

Ⓑ We did. We should screen them through their documents first.

★ **ōbosha** = applicant

2 皆さんは、大勢の中から<u>ふるいにかけられた</u>優秀な人ばかりで
_{みな} _{おおぜい} _{なか} _{ゆうしゅう} _{ひと}
す。ぜひ、わが社で力を発揮してください。
_{しゃ} _{ちから} _{はっき}

Mina-san wa, ōzē no naka kara furui ni kakerareta yūshū na hito bakari desu. Zehi, waga-sha de chikara o hakki shite kudasai.

You are all talented individuals, screened from a large pool. We would like you to show us what you can do at our company.

★ **hakki suru** = exert, show one's ability

切る to cut
_き

Useful One-word Expressions in Japanese 49

1. Switch off something, such as a machine.

2. To go under a certain number   3. To cut ties, to expire

Ex.1) エアコンを切る／電話を切る
_き _{でん わ} _き
To switch off an air conditioner/ to hang up (a telephone)

Ex.2) 1万円を切る
_{まんえん} _き
To cost less than \10,000

Ex.3) 彼との縁を切る／（自動詞で）契約が切れる
_{かれ} _{えん} _き _{じ どうし} _{けいやく} _き
To cut ties with him/ (intransitive verb) A contract expires

179 山のようにある
やま
Yama no yō ni aru

A lot; a mountain of

To have many of something. From the image of something stacked as high as a mountain. Used both for visible things as well as abstract things (tasks, jobs, and so on).

Listen & Speak

1 Ⓐ お先に失礼します。……まだ帰らないんですか。
さき　しつれい　　　　　　　　　　　　かえ
O-saki ni shitsurē shimasu. ...Mada kaeranai n desu ka?

Ⓑ 仕事が山のようにあってね。
しごと　やま
Shigoto ga yama no yō ni atte ne.

Ⓐ I'll be heading out. ...You're still not leaving?

Ⓑ I have a mountain of work to do.

★ **(o-)saki ni** = before you

2 Ⓐ 今月はクレームが山のようにあったな。
こんげつ　　　　　　　　やま
Kongetsu wa kurēmu ga yama no yō ni atta na.

Ⓑ そうでしたか。それはお疲れさまでした。
つか
Sō deshita ka. Sore wa o-tsukare-sama deshita.

Ⓐ We had a mountain of complaints this month.

Ⓑ Did you? That must have been tiring.

★ **kurēmu** = claim, complaints

山 mountain
やま

Useful One-word Expressions in Japanese 50

1. A lot of things piled up　2. An important stage, time

Ex.1)　ごみの山／書類の山／洗濯物の山
　　　　　　　　やま　しょるい　やま　せんたくもの　やま
　　A pile of rubbish ／A pile of documents／ A pile of dirty washing

Ex.2)　仕事が山を越えた。／今週が山だ。
　　　　しごと　やま　こ　　　　こんしゅう　やま
　　I finished that important job. ／This week is critical.

180 雲をつかむ
<ruby>雲<rt>くも</rt></ruby>を<ruby></ruby>つかむ
Kumo o tsukamu

Cloudy; indistinct

For something to be very obscure and unclear. The term comes from the indistinct nature of a cloud. Often followed by 「〜ような<ruby>話<rt>はなし</rt></ruby>」.

1 🅐 そんな<u>雲をつかむ</u>ような<ruby>話<rt>はなし</rt></ruby>じゃ、お<ruby>金<rt>かね</rt></ruby><ruby>出<rt>だ</rt></ruby>すわけにはいかないよ。

Sonna kumo o tsukamu yō na hanashi ja, o-kane dasu wake niwa ikanai yo.

🅑 そうですか……。

Sō desu ka ....

🅐 I'm not going to open my wallet for something that indistinct.

🅑 I see....

★ **~ wake niwa ikanai**
= there's no reason to ~, can't ~

2 🅐 <ruby>彼<rt>かれ</rt></ruby>、<ruby>仕事<rt>しごと</rt></ruby>やめる<ruby>理由<rt>りゆう</rt></ruby>、なんて<ruby>言<rt>い</rt></ruby>ってました？

Kare, shigoto yameru riyū, nante ittemashita?

🅑 それがよくわからないんだよ。<ruby>自分<rt>じぶん</rt></ruby>の<ruby>夢<rt>ゆめ</rt></ruby>がどうのって、<u>雲<rt>くも</rt>をつかむ</u>ような<ruby>話<rt>はなし</rt></ruby>でね。

Sore ga yoku wakaranai n da yo. Jibun no yume ga dō no tte, kumo o tsukamu yō na hanashi de ne.

🅐 Did he say why he was quitting his job?

🅑 I'm not sure. He said something indistinct about his dreams.

★ **yameru** = quit

Index (English version)
英語さくいん

Index
(English version)

Index (Japanese version)
日本語さくいん

S — Dazed, unfocused, unenthusiastic

T — Having a problem, undesired situation of result, tight situations

U — To be embarrassed, to be reflective

V — To endure, to withstand difficulty, to make a sacrifice, to take a risk

W — To be extremely surprised, to feel fear

X — Suffering a mishap, being betrayed, something going wrong

Y — Doing well and poorly, conditions going well and poorly

Z — Other

INDEX

● 著者

清ルミ Rumi Sei
常葉大学外国語学部教授。アメリカ国務省日本語研修所専任教官、ＮＨＫ教育テレビ日本語講座講師、EU-Japan Centre for Industrial Cooperation 日本言語文化研修責任者などを歴任。主な著書に『気持ちが伝わる日本語会話基本表現180』（Jリサーチ出版）、『優しい日本語——英語にできない「おかげさま」のこころ』『ナイフとフォークで冷奴——外国人には理解できない日本人の流儀』（以上、太陽出版）など。

本文レイアウト・DTP	オッコの木スタジオ
カバーデザイン	花本浩一
本文イラスト	藤井アキヒト
翻訳	Alex Ko Ransom ／ Caroline Q. Kuroda ／ Jenine Heaton
編集協力	髙橋尚子

日本人がよく使う 日本語会話お決まり表現 180

平成 29 年（2017 年）　1 月 10 日　初版第 1 刷発行
平成 30 年（2018 年）　4 月 10 日　　　第 2 刷発行

著　者	清ルミ	
発行人	福田富与	
発行所	有限会社Jリサーチ出版	
	〒166-0002　東京都杉並区高円寺北 2-29-14-705	
電　話	03(6808)8801（代）　FAX 03(5364)5310	
編集部	03(6808)8806	
	http://www.jresearch.co.jp	
印刷所	中央精版印刷株式会社	

ISBN 978-4-86392-325-6
禁無断転載。なお、乱丁、落丁はお取り替えいたします。

How to Download Voice Data

STEP 1	
Access the voice download website!	(Input the following URL:) **URL : http://febe.jp/jresearch**

STEP 2	
Continue to the FeBe registration page from the one displayed to register as a member.	Click 「FeBe に会員登録（無料）」 (Register to be a FeBe Member (Free)) ※ To download voice data, you must register for the FeBe audiobook delivery service (registration is free). Enter your email address, password (8 or more alphanumeric characters), name, birthday, and gender on the registration page ▶ Read the Terms of Service ▶ Click 「確認」(Confirm) ▶ Registration complete

STEP 3	
Return to the download page from the 「ご登録が完了しました」 page.	Click 「ダウンロードページ」 (Download Page), then enter "23256" in the field under 「シリアルコードをご入力ください」 (Please enter your serial code) on the page displayed and click 「送信」 (Send).

STEP 4	
Download voice data.	Click 「無料でオーディオブックを受け取る」 ▶ Click 「本棚で確認する」 ▶ Click 「ダウンロード」 (Download 「全体版」) ※ If you are using a PC, please download voice data from 「本棚」. If you are using a smartphone, a guide will appear for the FeBe app. Please use the voice files through the app.

⚠ Notice

- Voice data can be played from your PC, your iPhone, or your Android smartphone.
- Voice data can be downloaded and played as many times as you wish.
- For questions about downloads, please contact: info@febe.jp (Emails will be received from 10 AM to 8 PM on weekdays).